# Hands-On Math

## Learning Numeration
## through Manipulative Activities
### 2nd edition

By
Dr. Kathleen Fletcher-Bacer

Order this book online at www.trafford.com/07-1947
or email orders@trafford.com

Most Trafford titles are also available at major online book retailers.

Note for Librarians: A cataloguing record for this book is available from Library and Archives Canada at www.collectionscanada.ca/amicus/index-e.html

Printed in Victoria, BC, Canada.

ISBN: 978-1-4251-4575-0

*We at Trafford believe that it is the responsibility of us all, as both individuals and corporations, to make choices that are environmentally and socially sound. You, in turn, are supporting this responsible conduct each time you purchase a Trafford book, or make use of our publishing services. To find out how you are helping, please visit www.trafford.com/responsiblepublishing.html*

*Our mission is to efficiently provide the world's finest, most comprehensive book publishing service, enabling every author to experience success. To find out how to publish your book, your way, and have it available worldwide, visit us online at www.trafford.com/10510*

www.trafford.com

**North America & international**
toll-free: 1 888 232 4444 (USA & Canada)
phone: 250 383 6864 ♦ fax: 250 383 6804
email: info@trafford.com

**The United Kingdom & Europe**
phone: +44 (0)1865 722 113 ♦ local rate: 0845 230 9601
facsimile: +44 (0)1865 722 868 ♦ email: info.uk@trafford.com

10 9 8 7 6 5 4 3 2

# Table of Contents

## Numeration Activities through 100,000,000,000

# ABOUT THIS BOOK

I hear and I forget.
I see and I remember.
I do and I understand.
Chinese Proverb

*Hands-On Math* is based on this proverb. The use of manipulatives is the key to enabling students to understand abstract mathematical concepts. With the National Council of Teachers of Mathematics' Standards (NCTM) serving as a model for what should be occurring in mathematics classrooms, manipulatives are now essential. Learning how to use manipulatives in the classroom, however, is challenging. It is very important to use manipulatives in the manner they are designed – to develop those very important foundational mathematical concepts throughout the grade levels, thus making mathematics understandable to children. It has been my experience that children who discover foundational mathematical concepts for themselves retain those concepts and are able to transfer them beautifully to higher levels of mathematics. If the manipulatives are not presented in the correct manner, they may serve to confuse the student rather than enhance learning.

The purpose of this book is to provide the teacher with a realistic approach to teaching with manipulatives. Use the activities to teach and develop the foundational skill and then utilize the manipulatives right along with textbook and supportive materials.

Activities that focus on numeration provide the core of this book. Numeration is a key concept in developing number sense. Number sense, as defined by the National Council of Teachers of Mathematics, is: (1) understanding the meaning of numbers; (2) having an awareness of multiple relationships among numbers; (3) recognizing the magnitude of numbers; (4) knowing the relative effects of operating on numbers; and (5) possessing referents for measures of common objects and situations in the environment (NCTM 1989, p. 38). Many of these concepts will be addressed throughout this book.

The book is divided into specific skill categories. Each activity includes the skill in parenthesis in the table of contents. When you are in need of a lesson plan or a math activity for your students, simply choose one suited to the skill you are teaching.

The ⚘ symbol identifies the teacher pages. Each of these pages outlines a manipulative lesson for you to follow. Quite often, a student page accompanies a teacher page so that the concept may be strengthened by student practice.

Each page, labeled with a ✎ symbol invites students to investigate a concept. These student pages are best used initially with the teacher's direction. Once underway, however, student pages may be completed individually, minimizing teacher involvement.

# Numeration Activities through 100

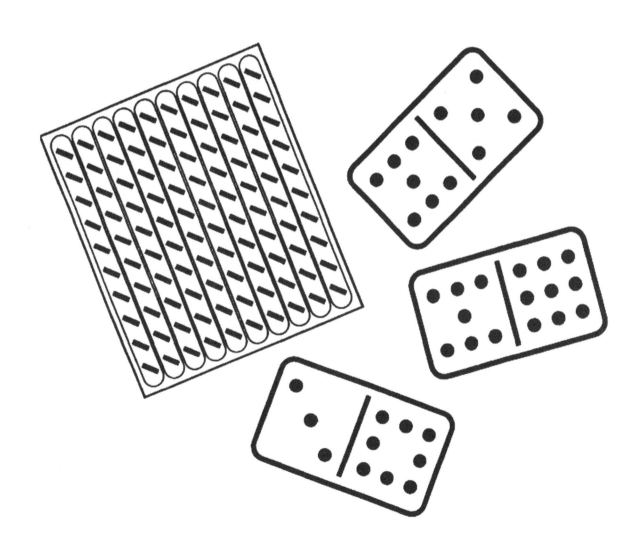

 NUMERATION CONCEPT:
*Understanding the numbers 1-10*

# Shapes and Stamps

**Preparation:**
- Select a variety of rubber stamps, stickers, or small cutout shapes.

- Distribute to each student a black felt-tip marker, 12"x18" white construction paper and glue

- Supply stamp pads (if using stamps).

**Procedure:**
- Draw lines, as shown below, to divide the construction paper into ten sections. In each section, write a number from 1-10 in random order.

| | | | | |
|---|---|---|---|---|
| 1 | 4 | 2 | 8 | 5 |
| 3 | 7 | 10 | 9 | 6 |

- Distribute stamps, sticker, or cutout shapes to the students.

- Allow the students to stamp, stick, or glue the correct number of objects in each section.

- You may also use this activity as a learning center in the classroom.

# Seven-Up

## Preparation:
- Arrange a large area in the classroom where the students can sit in a circle

## Procedure:
- Ask the students to sit in a large circle.

- Begin by having students count from one to seven with each student speaking a number (the direction of the counting is around the circle, clockwise or counterclockwise, without skipping any students)

- When a student says, "seven" he or she stands up. The next student will begin with number one again. Play continues until every student is standing. Repeat this activity with other numbers from 3-10.

## Variation/Extensions:

- Have all students begin by standing. Each student will sit when a specific number is called.

- Have students to predict which student will be the next to either stand or sit.

# NUMERATION CONCEPT:
## *Understanding sets with 1-12 members*

# Unifix™ It to 12

## Preparation:

- Supply each student with twelve Unifix™ cubes of various colors

- Distribute a copy of page 12 to each student

- Students will need crayons the same colors as the unifix™ cubes.

## Procedure:

- Ask each student to select one Unifix™ cube.

- Using the worksheet on page 12, the student will color the first square the same color as the Unifix™ cube he or she selected.

- Have the student return the Unifix™ cube to their pile of cubes and randomly select two Unifix™ cubes. Sometimes students like to close their eyes as they pick.

- The student then colors two squares on page 12 to match the cubes selected. The student continues the activity to 12.

## Extension:

- Distribute a copy of page 13 to each student. The numbers 1-12 appear in random order. The student will draw the number of Unifix™ cubes that correspond to the graph on page 13. The student will color the squares to match the cubes that were selected.

# Unifix it to 12

| 1 | | | | | | | | | | | | |
|---|---|---|---|---|---|---|---|---|---|---|---|---|
| 2 | | | | | | | | | | | | |
| 3 | | | | | | | | | | | | |
| 4 | | | | | | | | | | | | |
| 5 | | | | | | | | | | | | |
| 6 | | | | | | | | | | | | |
| 7 | | | | | | | | | | | | |
| 8 | | | | | | | | | | | | |
| 9 | | | | | | | | | | | | |
| 10 | | | | | | | | | | | | |
| 11 | | | | | | | | | | | | |
| 12 | | | | | | | | | | | | |

Name_____ Date_____

# Unifix it to 12

| 5 | | | | | | | | | | | |
|----|--|--|--|--|--|--|--|--|--|--|--|
| 7 | | | | | | | | | | | |
| 12 | | | | | | | | | | | |
| 3 | | | | | | | | | | | |
| 4 | | | | | | | | | | | |
| 2 | | | | | | | | | | | |
| 8 | | | | | | | | | | | |
| 10 | | | | | | | | | | | |
| 9 | | | | | | | | | | | |
| 11 | | | | | | | | | | | |
| 6 | | | | | | | | | | | |
| 1 | | | | | | | | | | | |

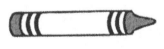

Name_____ Date_____

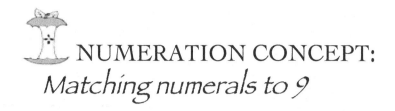

# NUMERATION CONCEPT:
## *Matching numerals to 9*

# Domino It!

## Preparation:
- Supply each student with double-six or double-nine domino set.

- If commercially made dominoes are not available, patterns for Double-Six and Double-Nine dominoes can be found on pages 15-16. Copy the patterns on cardstock, cut out the sets, and place the sets in reclosable bags. If you copy the sets on different colored cardstock or number the sets on the back, this will help keep the sets from getting mixed up with the other sets.

- Each student will need a **Domino It** worksheet.
  Page 17 requires a Double-Six set of dominoes and develops the numbers 0-6
  Page 18 requires a Double-Nine set of dominoes and develops the numbers 0-9

## Procedure:
- Ask each student to select a domino that matches a domino found on his or her **Domino It!** worksheet

- The student places the actual domino on top of the domino printed on the worksheet.

- As the student o record the number of dots found on the top portion of the domino on the first line. The student will also record the number of dots found on the bottom portion of the domino on the second line.

## Extension:

- Students can design problems for each other using page 19. Permit one student to design a **Domino It**! Page for another student to solve.

- If you want to extend the activity to numerals up to 12 (Double-Six set) or 18 (Double-Nine set) have them count the total number of dots on one domino and record that numeral.

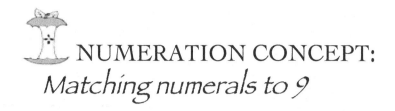

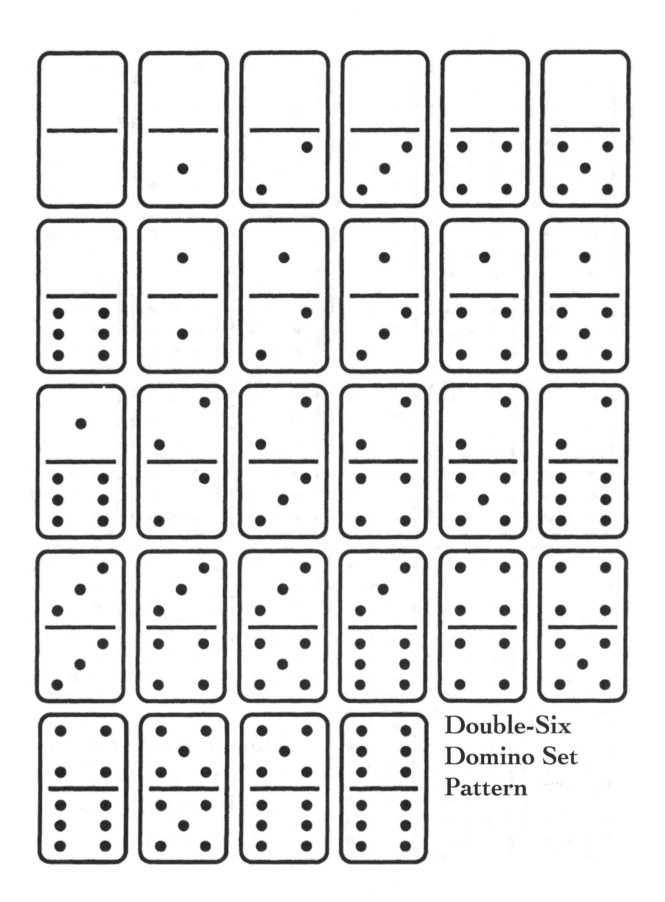

Double-Six
Domino Set
Pattern

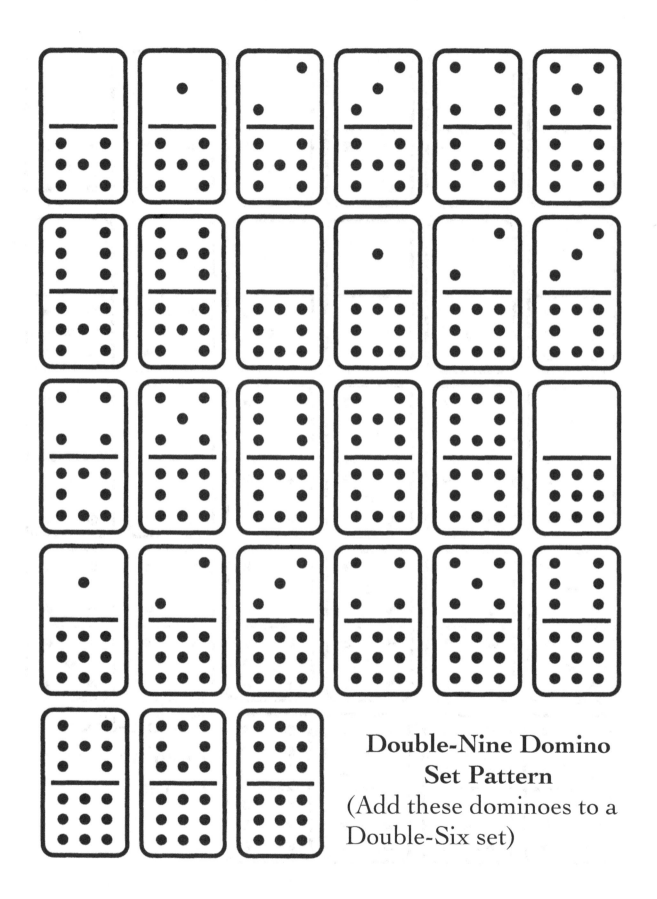

**Double-Nine Domino
Set Pattern**
(Add these dominoes to a
Double-Six set)

# Domino It!

Find the domino that matches each picture. Place it on the domino picture. Record the number of dots on the top and the bottom of each domino.

1. = __3__

   = __4__

2. = __

   = __

3. = __

   = __

4. = __

   = __

5. = __

   = __

6. = __

   = __

7. = __

   = __

8. = __

   = __

9. = __

   = __

10. = __

    = __

11. = __

    = __

12. = __

    = __

Name_____ Date_____

# Domino It!

Find the domino that matches each picture. Place it on the domino picture. Record the number of dots on the top and the bottom of each domino.

**1.** = __0__
    = __7__

**2.** = ___
    = ___

**3.** = ___
    = ___

**4.** = ___
    = ___

**5.** = ___
    = ___

**6.** = ___
    = ___

**7.** = ___
    = ___

**8.** = ___
    = ___

**9.** = ___
    = ___

**10.** = ___
    = ___

**11.** = ___
    = ___

**12.** = ___
    = ___

Name_____ Date_____

# Domino It!

Make a *Domino It!* page for a friend. Draw dots on each domino below. Ask a classmate to record the correct number of dots found on each domino.

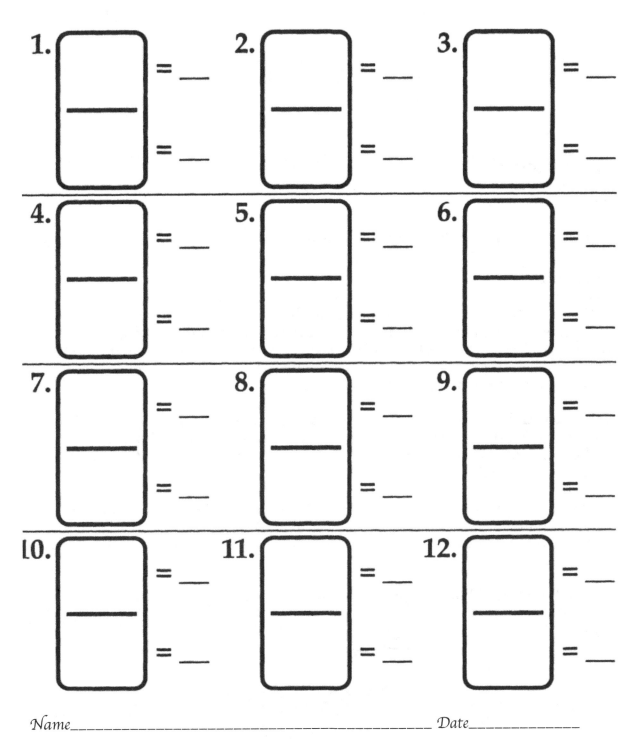

1. ___ = __

   = __

2. ___ = __

   = __

3. ___ = __

   = __

4. ___ = __

   = __

5. ___ = __

   = __

6. ___ = __

   = __

7. ___ = __

   = __

8. ___ = __

   = __

9. ___ = __

   = __

10. ___ = __

    = __

11. ___ = __

    = __

12. ___ = __

    = __

Name_____ Date_____

NUMERATION CONCEPT:
*Reinforcing the concept of 10 and its multiples*

# Beanstick Factory

## Preparation:
- Provide students with popsicle sticks (older students) or tongue depressors (younger students).

- Provide an ample supply of kidney beans and glue.

## Procedure:
- Instruct each student to make a beanstick using ten beans. Apply glue liberally to the stick. Place ten beans in the glue on the stick. Follow with a final coat of glue in between and over the tops of the beans. This will prevent slipping. Allow the beansticks to dry for 24 hours. If a beanstick contains more than or fewer than ten beans (by accident), ask the students," How many more (or fewer) beans do we need to make a ten-bean stick?"

- To work with larger numbers, allow the students to make 100-bean flats. Place ten beansticks side by side onto heavy tag board. Glue the beansticks together and put a final coat of glue over the top. A pattern for additional 100-bean flats is shown on page 21.

- Have students create a beanstick kit. The kit should contain one or two 100-bean flats, nine beansticks, and 21 loose beans. Place each kit in a reclosable bag. Use these kits to discuss place value, or ask the students to model specific numbers.

- Page 22 can be used to get students started on the pictorial representation of numbers.

# Beansticks
# Hundred-Bean Flats

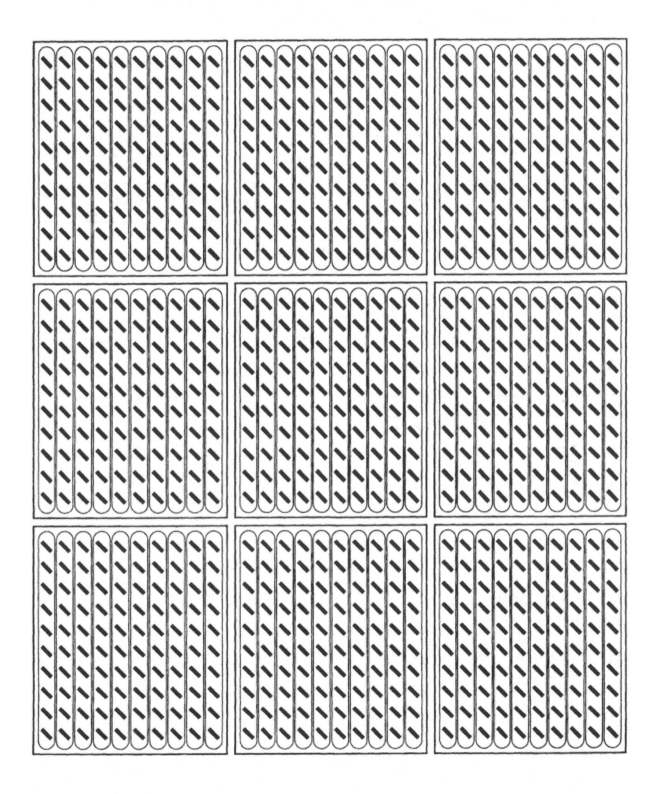

# Beansticks

Look at the beansticks below. Add or subtract beans to complete each beanstick.
Remember, each beanstick should contain 10 beans.

Example:

|  | Beans here | Add or Subtract | Draw beansticks here |
|---|---|---|---|
| **A:** | ꝺꝺꝺꝺꝺꝺꝺꝺ | ♡ ♡ | ꝺꝺꝺꝺꝺꝺꝺꝺꝺꝺ |
| **B:** | ꝺꝺꝺꝺꝺꝺꝺꝺꝺꝺꝺ | ⊗ | ꝺꝺꝺꝺꝺꝺꝺꝺꝺꝺ |
| **1.** | ꝺ ꝺ ꝺ ꝺ ꝺ ꝺ ꝺ | | |
| **2.** | ꝺꝺꝺꝺꝺꝺꝺꝺꝺꝺꝺꝺ | | |
| **3.** | ꝺ ꝺ ꝺ ꝺ ꝺ ꝺ | | |
| **4.** | ꝺꝺꝺꝺꝺꝺꝺꝺꝺꝺ | | |
| **5.** | ꝺꝺꝺꝺꝺꝺꝺꝺꝺ | | |
| **6.** | ꝺ ꝺ ꝺ ꝺ | | |
| **7.** | ꝺꝺꝺꝺꝺꝺꝺꝺꝺꝺꝺ | | |
| **8.** | ꝺꝺꝺꝺꝺꝺꝺꝺꝺꝺꝺ | | |
| **9.** | ꝺꝺꝺꝺꝺꝺꝺꝺ | | |

# NUMERATION CONCEPT:
## Counting Numbers to 50

# Counting Numbers

## Preparation:

• Distribute 50 beans and five small cups to each student or groups of students.

• Copy the place value mat on page 24 for each student or group of students. If a larger mat is needed, divide a large sheet of construction paper into three equal parts. Label the sections as follows: Hundreds, Tens, and Ones.

## Procedure:

• Place a place value mat in front of the student (or group). Begin counting out beans and place them on the mat. When you reach ten, ask the student (or group) to place the ten beans into a cup. Emphasize that you cannot have ten beans in the ones column. Ask the student to place the cup in the tens column.

• Continue counting until 50 beans are counted out. Each time a multiple of ten is reached, ask the student (or group) to place the beans in the cup and move it to the tens column. Stop periodically and ask the student how many beans are displayed on the mat. Ask the student to write the number of beans that are displayed. Keep the emphasis on place value by asking the student to state how many tens and ones are displayed.

• This can also be done easily using an overhead projector and as a class activity.

# Place Value Mat

| Hundreds | Tens | Ones |
|---|---|---|

# NUMERATION CONCEPT:
## Counting Numbers to 100

# Paper Chains

## Preparation:

- Cut colored construction paper into 1"x6" strips.

- Distribute glue (or staplers) and markers to students.

## Procedure:

- Demonstrate to the students how to make a paper chain. Glue (or staple) the ends of a construction-paper strip together. Thread another strip through the first loop and glue (or staple) the ends of the second strip together.

- As the students attach each loop, instruct them to write the numbers 1-100 on the loops, one number per loop.

- Permit students to work together to form a paper chain that reaches around the room.

## Extension:

- Create a "Make-A-Chain" Activity center for each student to make an individual chain for additional reinforcement.

 NUMERATION CONCEPT:
*Understanding the numbers 1-100*

# Hundred-Board Activities

## Preparation:

- Cover a bulletin board with paper. Make a grid by dividing the paper with ten columns and ten rows. This will create 100 small squares.

- Write the numerals 1-100 on round tags. Using thumbtacks, place each numbered tag consecutively on the grid.

## Procedure:

- After the students have seen the hundred-board, turn each-tag numeral over. When this is done, students will not be able to see the numerals.

- Turn over one numeral in each row and ask the students to state or write the numeral.

## Variations:

- Other ideas of ways to use the number board are:
  - o Turn over groups of three consecutive numbers in a row.
  - o Turn over an entire row
  - o Turn over every other row
  - o Turn over four rows
  Each time have the students state or write the numerals that you point to

- When all of the numerals are showing, begin turning over various patterns of numbers. Ask the students to state or write which numerals are now hidden.

- After this activity has been introduced to students, permit them to conduct these activities in small groups, with one student playing the role of the teacher for each group.

# NUMERATION CONCEPT:
## *Understanding numbers to 50*

# Building Two-Digit Numerals

## Preparation:

- Distribute beanstick kits or base-ten blocks. (See page 20 for beanstick kits).

- Distribute a place value mat (Use pattern on page 24).

## Procedure:

- Ask the student to place four beans (units or cubes) in the ones column of the place value mat. Add five more beans to the ones column. Have the student count the total number of beans (9). Instruct the student to add one more bean to the ones column. At this point the student will trade the group of ten beans for 1 ten stick. (If the student is using based ten blocks, the student will trade the ten units for a rod of ten units).

- Continue adding beans to the place value mat. Periodically stop and ask the student to describe the number that is represented on the mat. How many ones are there? How many tense are in the number?

## Variations:

- Another way to assess the student's comprehension of the concept of place value is to ask the student to display a specific number with the manipulatives. Question the student by asking how many tens (or ones) are in a particular number.

# NUMERATION CONCEPT:
## *Understanding numbers to 99*

# Spinning Two-Digit Numbers

## Preparation:

* Distribute beanstick kits (see page 20) or base ten blocks and a place value mat (see page 24).

* Create an overhead spinner with the digits 0-9 on it. (Refer to the pattern on page 29).

## Procedure:

* Spin the overhead spinner. Ask the student to place the number spun in the ones column. Spin again and instruct the student to place that number of tens on the mat. The student will then read the number that was created.

* Using a beanstick kit or base ten blocks, ask each student to show a specific number on his or her mat. Repeat this activity naming larger two-digit numbers. Continue this activity until the student can represent the numbers with ease. To move the student into a more abstract representation of this concept, assign pages 30-31.

* Permit the students to work in groups of two. One student sets up the mat and the other student reads the number displayed. Swap roles and continue playing.

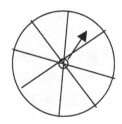

| Tens | Ones |
|------|------|

2

# Overhead Spinner

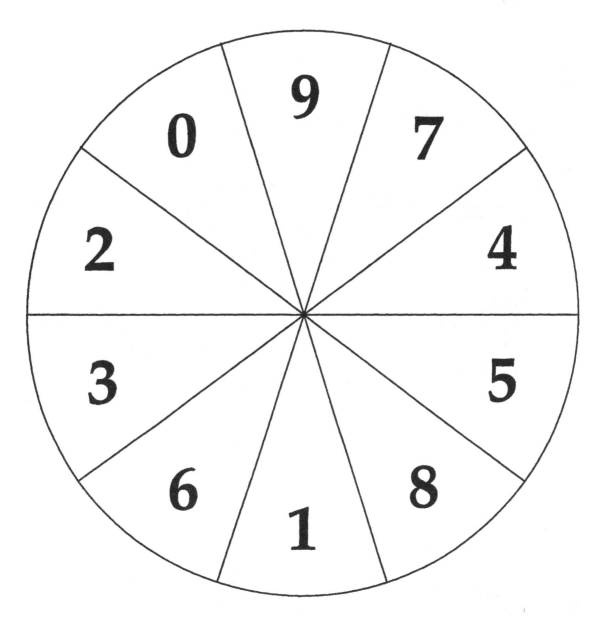

To make an overhead spinner, copy the pattern onto a transparency. Thread a brad through the small circle of a safety pin and then through the transparency. The safety pin becomes the spinner!

# Understanding Numbers to 99

Write the numeral that is displayed in each illustration.

**1.** <u>23</u>

**2.** _____

**3.** _____

**4.** _____

**5.** _____

**6.** _____

**7.** _____

**8.** _____

**9.** _____

Name_____ Date_____

# Understanding Numbers to 99

Write the numeral that is displayed in each illustration.

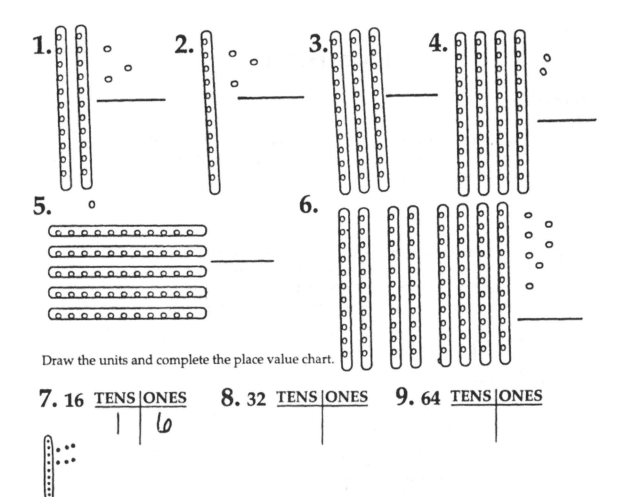

1. _____

2. _____

3. _____

4. _____

5. _____

6. _____

Draw the units and complete the place value chart.

7. 16 | TENS | ONES
   |  1  |  6

8. 32 | TENS | ONES

9. 64 | TENS | ONES

10. 21 | TENS | ONES

11. 72 | TENS | ONES

Name_____ Date_____

# NUMERATION CONCEPT:
## *Writing two-digit numerals*

# Domino It!

## Preparation:

- Create or purchase overhead transparency dominoes. For teacher-made dominoes, copy the domino patters from pages 15-16 onto a transparency. Cut out the transparency dominoes

## Procedure:

- Using the overhead dominoes, discuss how the two portions of the dominoes could represent the place value positions of tens and ones. Place several dominoes on the overhead and demonstrate how they could be read. For example, this domino could represent 24, or 2 tens and 4 ones.

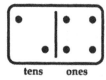

- After the students understand how the dominoes are to be read, ask the students to find the domino with the following characteristics:
  - ➢ a 3 in the tens place and a 6 in the ones place
  - ➢ a 4 in the tens place and a 2 in the ones place
  - ➢ a 5 in the tens place and a 0 in the ones place
  - ➢ a 1 in the tens place and a 1 in the ones place
  - ➢ a 6 in the tens place and a 6 in the ones place
  - ➢ a 3 in the tens place and a 1 in the ones place
  - ➢ a 2 in the tens place and a 6 in the ones place
  - ➢ a 0 in the tens place and a 2 in the ones place
  - ➢ a 6 in the tens place and a 5 in the ones place

- Distribute page 33 and a set of Double-Nine dominoes to each student. (Teacher-made dominoes may be made by copying pages 15-16 onto cardstock)

- Page 34 allows the students to design problems for other students to solve. Distribute this page if additional practice is needed.

# Writing Two-Digit Numerals

Find the correct domino for each problem. Copy the domino onto the pattern and write the numeral it represents. The first problem has been done for you.

1. 8 in the tens place, 6 in the ones place
2. 1 in the tens place, 7 in the ones place
3. 8 in the tens place, 5 in the ones place
4. 9 in the tens place, 2 in the ones place
5. 5 in the tens place, 9 in the ones place
6. 2 in the tens place, 3 in the ones place
7. 3 in the tens place, 8 in the ones place
8. 7 in the tens place, 7 in the ones place
9. 4 in the tens place, 8 in the ones place

**1. Tens   Ones**

86

**2. Tens   Ones**

_____

**3. Tens   Ones**

_____

**4. Tens   Ones**

_____

**5. Tens   Ones**

_____

**6. Tens   Ones**

_____

**7. Tens   Ones**

_____

**8. Tens   Ones**

_____

**9. Tens   Ones**

_____

Name_____ Date_____

# Writing Two-Digit Numerals

Use a set of dominoes to design problems for your friend to solve.

1. _____     6. _____

2. _____     7. _____

3. _____     8. _____

4. _____     9. _____

5. _____

Example:

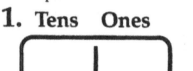

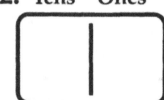

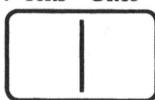

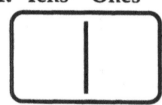

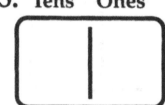

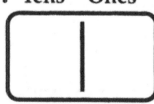

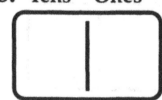

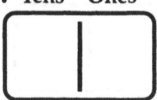

Name_____ Date_____

# Numeration Activities through 1,000

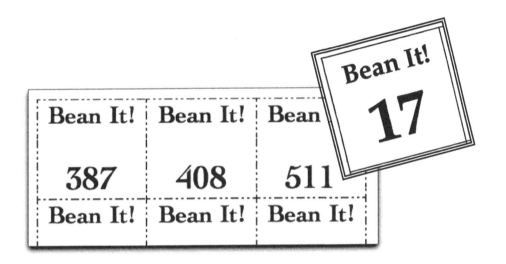

| Bean It! | Bean It! | Bean It! | **Bean It!** |
|---|---|---|---|
| 387 | 408 | 511 | **17** |
| Bean It! | Bean It! | Bean It! | |

| Up & Down | Up & Down | Up & Down | Up & Down |
|---|---|---|---|
| 93 | 94 | 95 | 96 |
| The River | The River | The River | The River |
| Up & Down | Up & Down | Up & Down | Up & Down |
| 97 | 98 | 99 | 100 |
| The River | The River | The River | The River |

# Building Numerals

## Preparation:
- Distribute a beanstick kit to each student (page 20). The student will need additional 100-bean flats. An illustration of 100-bean flats can be found on page 21. Base ten blocks can be substituted for the beanstick kit.

- Distribute a place value mat (page 24) to each student.

## Procedure:
- Ask the student to display four beansticks and seven loose beans. Ask the student, "How many beans are displayed all together?" (47).

- Reverse the activity by asking the student to display 73 beans. Ask the student, "How many beansticks are in the model?" (7). "How many beans are in the model?" (3).

- When the student learns to consistently represent the correct numbers, introduce the hundred-bean flat. Begin asking the student to represent numbers to 999. Be certain that he or she is not placing more than nine manipulatives in the ones or tens column.

- For additional practice, place the students in pairs. One student displays a number on the place value mat with the manipulatives. The other student, using page 38, records the actual number shown by the first student.

# Building Numerals

| 1. | Hundreds | Tens | Ones |
|---|---|---|---|
| | □ | □ | □ |
| | | | |

| 2. | Hundreds | Tens | Ones |
|---|---|---|---|
| | □ | □ | □ |
| | | | |

| 3. | Hundreds | Tens | Ones |
|---|---|---|---|
| | □ | □ | □ |
| | | | |

| 4. | Hundreds | Tens | Ones |
|---|---|---|---|
| | □ | □ | □ |
| | | | |

| 5. | Hundreds | Tens | Ones |
|---|---|---|---|
| | □ | □ | □ |
| | | | |

| 6. | Hundreds | Tens | Ones |
|---|---|---|---|
| | □ | □ | □ |
| | | | |

| 7. | Hundreds | Tens | Ones |
|---|---|---|---|
| | □ | □ | □ |
| | | | |

| 8. | Hundreds | Tens | Ones |
|---|---|---|---|
| | □ | □ | □ |
| | | | |

Name _____   Date _____

# NUMERATION CONCEPT:
*Developing the relationship between concrete & symbolic representation*

# Double Show Me

## Preparation:
* Make a Place Value Flip Card for each student or groups of students (see instructions below).

* Distribute a beanstick kit or the base ten blocks to each student (for information on beanstick kits see page 20).

* Distribute place value mat to each student (pattern, page 24).

* Overhead projector , Overhead base ten pieces

## To make a Place Value Flip Card

Each student will need the following materials:
* One  7" x 11" piece of heavy tag board, marker

* three metal rings (1"size), hole punch

* thirty unlined (3"x 5") index cards (for each Place Value Flip Card you will need ten cards in each of the following colors: yellow, blue, and green).

## Construction:
Ask each student to separate the index card into three sets, by color. Have the students label the cards in each set 0-9. Divide the tag board into three equal sections and punch a hole in the center of each section. Label the sections in place value order (hundreds, tens, and ones).

Punch a whole in the center of each card. Arrange the cards in consecutive order. Thread the ring through the cards. For example, the green cards will be placed under the section marked hundreds. Thread the ring through the index cards and then through the tag board. Follow the same procedure for the tens place and the ones place (see diagram on page 40).

*Place Value Flip card*

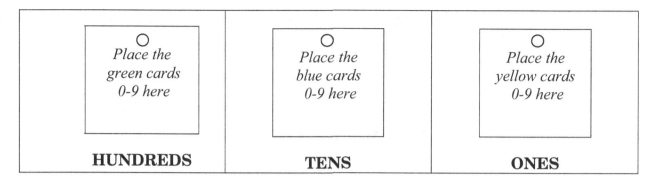

| HUNDREDS | TENS | ONES |
|---|---|---|
| ◯ *Place the green cards 0-9 here* | ◯ *Place the blue cards 0-9 here* | ◯ *Place the yellow cards 0-9 here* |

## Procedure:

- Begin the activity by asking the students to "Show me" one ten and seven ones using the place value manipulatives.

- Using the overhead projector, model the number with the manipulatives. Continue the activity using a variety of three-digit numbers. After several examples begin "Double Show Me."

- Play "Double Show Me" by calling out a number. The students first create the number using their place value materials. Then the students finish with a "Double Show Me" by showing the numeral on their Place Value Flip Charts.

# NUMERATION CONCEPT:
*Developing the relationship between representation & the symbolic with three-digit numerals*

# Draw It – Write It

## Preparation:
• Reproduce page 42 for each student.

## Procedure:
• On the whiteboard/overhead, draw the key shown below:

= 1 hundred (100)

= 1 ten (10)

= one (1)

• Distribute copies of page 42 to the students.

• Call out various numbers and ask the students to use the symbols drawn on the blackboard to draw the numbers on their worksheet in the spaces marked "Draw Here."

• Ask students to use their pictures of the numbers to record the numerical value in the spaces market "Write Here."

# Draw It- Write It

| | □ | ▭ | ▫ |
|---|---|---|---|
| **1.** Draw Here | | | |
| Write Here | | | |
| **2.** Draw Here | | | |
| Write Here | | | |
| **3.** Draw Here | | | |
| Write Here | | | |
| **4.** Draw Here | | | |
| Write Here | | | |
| **5.** Draw Here | | | |
| Write Here | | | |
| **6.** Draw Here | | | |
| Write Here | | | |
| **7.** Draw Here | | | |
| Write Here | | | |

Name _____ Date _____

# NUMERATION CONCEPT:
## *Representing three-digit numerals with physical objects*

# Bean It!

## Preparation:
• Reproduce page 42 for each student.

## Procedure:
• Divide the students into groups of four. Assign the following roles: hundred counter, ten counter, one counter, and checker.

• Distribute the materials to each group.

• Instruct all students to place their hands in their laps.

• Draw a card from the deck, display the number or call it out, and say, "Bean It!"

• The hundreds counter places the correct number of 100-bean flats in the hundreds area of the Place Value Construction Board. The tens counter places the correct number of beansticks in the tens area. The ones counter places the correct number of beans in the ones area of the board. The checker verifies the physical model of the number and then raises his or her hand.

• The first group to display the number correctly scores a point. Game continues until a group scores 10 points.

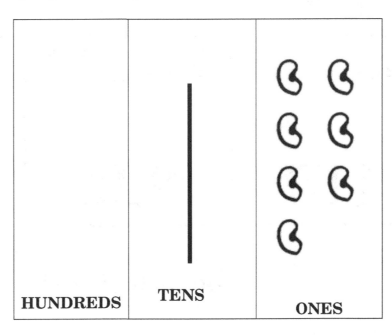

| Bean It! | Bean It! | Bean It! |
|:---:|:---:|:---:|
| 17 | 23 | 47 |
| Bean It! | Bean It! | Bean It! |
| 51 | 68 | 70 |
| Bean It! | Bean It! | Bean It! |
| 89 | 92 | 101 |
| Bean It! | Bean It! | Bean It! |
| 118 | 222 | 337 |

**Bean It! Cards**

| Bean It! | Bean It! | Bean It! |
|---|---|---|
| 387 | 408 | 511 |
| Bean It! | Bean It! | Bean It! |
| 641 | 773 | 828 |
| Bean It! | Bean It! | Bean It! |
| 916 | 973 | 4 |
| Bean It! | Bean It! | Bean It! |
| 369 | 187 | 234 |

Bean It! Cards

# NUMERATION CONCEPT:
## Counting from 0 to 999

# Flip Chart Counting

### Preparation:
- Distribute Place Value Flip Charts (instructions on page 39).

- You will need an overhead spinner with digits 0-9 on it (see instructions, pages 28-29).

### Procedure:

- Ask the students to turn their Place Value Flip Charts to  Begin counting aloud with the students (1,2,3,4,5,6,7,8,9,1 ten, 2 tens, etc...). Continue counting with them, physically moving the cards on the Place Value Flip Chart.

- Starting at , ask students to flip their charts to show each next numeral. Allow the students to discover that they are adding one each time. Periodically, change the starting number and continue asking the students to say the next number.

- Spin the overhead spinner. Ask the students to show the numeral on the spinner with their Place Value Flip Chart. For example, if the spinner lands on 9, all students show 9 on their Place Value Flip Chart. Spin the spinner again. If the spinner lands on 2, ask students to show you 2 more on their Place Value Flip Chart. The students should then flip the cards to the number 11 (9 + 2 = 11), Continue this procedure until the students show that they have mastered this activity.

- Choose a textbook and open it to any page. Call out the page number to the students. Ask the students to represent the page number using their Place Value Flip Charts.

NUMERATION CONCEPT:
*Ordering numerals 1-100*

# Up and Down the River

## Preparation:

• Prepare a set of Up and Down the River Cards for each group of six students (pattern on pages 48-56).

## Procedure:

• Divide the students into groups of six ad distribute a set of cards to each group.

• Ask one student in each group to shuffle the cards and deal them evenly among the members of the group.

• Students are to look at their cards, but they are not to show them to each other.

• Suggest to the students that they should order their cards from smallest to largest

• Whoever holds the 1 card plays first. He or she should lay down the card and say, "One."

• Play continues with cards 2,3,4,etc., until 100 is reached.

• The object of the game is to play a card quickly and to keep the game going without any pauses.

• Shuffle and deal the cards again and go "down the river" by starting with 100 and counting backwards.

• Whenever there is a pause (15 seconds or more), the student holding the card that should be been played receives a point. The lowest score wins.

# Up and Down the River

| Up & Down **1** The River | Up & Down **2** The River | Up & Down **3** The River | Up & Down **4** The River |
|---|---|---|---|
| Up & Down **5** The River | Up & Down **6** The River | Up & Down **7** The River | Up & Down **8** The River |

| Up & Down | Up & Down | Up & Down | Up & Down |
|---|---|---|---|
| **9** | **10** | **11** | **12** |
| The River | The River | The River | The River |
| Up & Down | Up & Down | Up & Down | Up & Down |
| **13** | **14** | **15** | **16** |
| The River | The River | The River | The River |
| Up & Down | Up & Down | Up & Down | Up & Down |
| **17** | **18** | **19** | **20** |
| The River | The River | The River | The River |

| | | | |
|---|---|---|---|
| Up & Down **21** The River | Up & Down **22** The River | Up & Down **23** The River | Up & Down **24** The River |
| Up & Down **25** The River | Up & Down **26** The River | Up & Down **27** The River | Up & Down **28** The River |
| Up & Down **29** The River | Up & Down **30** The River | Up & Down **31** The River | Up & Down **32** The River |

| Up & Down | Up & Down | Up & Down | Up & Down |
|---|---|---|---|
| **33** | **34** | **35** | **36** |
| The River | The River | The River | The River |
| Up & Down | Up & Down | Up & Down | Up & Down |
| **37** | **38** | **39** | **40** |
| The River | The River | The River | The River |
| Up & Down | Up & Down | Up & Down | Up & Down |
| **41** | **42** | **43** | **44** |
| The River | The River | The River | The River |

| | | | |
|---|---|---|---|
| Up & Down **45** The River | Up & Down **46** The River | Up & Down **47** The River | Up & Down **48** The River |
| Up & Down **49** The River | Up & Down **50** The River | Up & Down **51** The River | Up & Down **52** The River |
| Up & Down **53** The River | Up & Down **54** The River | Up & Down **55** The River | Up & Down **56** The River |

| | | | |
|---|---|---|---|
| Up & Down<br><br>**57**<br><br>The River | Up & Down<br><br>**58**<br><br>The River | Up & Down<br><br>**59**<br><br>The River | Up & Down<br><br>**60**<br><br>The River |
| Up & Down<br><br>**61**<br><br>The River | Up & Down<br><br>**62**<br><br>The River | Up & Down<br><br>**63**<br><br>The River | Up & Down<br><br>**64**<br><br>The River |
| Up & Down<br><br>**65**<br><br>The River | Up & Down<br><br>**66**<br><br>The River | Up & Down<br><br>**67**<br><br>The River | Up & Down<br><br>**68**<br><br>The River |

| Up & Down | Up & Down | Up & Down | Up & Down |
|:---:|:---:|:---:|:---:|
| **69** | **70** | **71** | **72** |
| The River | The River | The River | The River |
| Up & Down | Up & Down | Up & Down | Up & Down |
| **73** | **74** | **75** | **76** |
| The River | The River | The River | The River |
| Up & Down | Up & Down | Up & Down | Up & Down |
| **77** | **78** | **79** | **80** |
| The River | The River | The River | The River |

| Up & Down | Up & Down | Up & Down | Up & Down |
|---|---|---|---|
| **81** | **82** | **83** | **84** |
| The River | The River | The River | The River |
| Up & Down | Up & Down | Up & Down | Up & Down |
| **85** | **86** | **87** | **88** |
| The River | The River | The River | The River |
| Up & Down | Up & Down | Up & Down | Up & Down |
| **89** | **90** | **91** | **92** |
| The River | The River | The River | The River |

| Up & Down 93 The River | Up & Down 94 The River | Up & Down 95 The River | Up & Down 96 The River |
|---|---|---|---|
| Up & Down 97 The River | Up & Down 98 The River | Up & Down 99 The River | Up & Down 100 The River |

# Order It to Go!

## Preparation:

- A pair of standard dice can be used for set A, but for all the other sets use blank wooden dice to create the other sets by writing the numbers with permanent pens.

  **Set A -** 1,2,3,4,5,6          **Set E –** 1,3,5,7,9,9
  **Set B –** 4,5,6,7,8,9          **Set F –** 1,1,3,3,5,5
  **Set C -** 1,2,3,5,6,7          **Set G –** 0,2,4,6,8,8
  **Set D –** 0,2,4,5,7,9          **Set H –** 2,2,4,6,8,8

- Reproduce the **Order It to Go** recording sheet (page 59) so that each student has a copy.

## Procedure:

- Place students in small groups.

- The six dice in each group are thrown. Each student records the resulting six numbers on the **Order It to Go** recording sheet.

- The students then record the three different numerals in the second column of the recording sheet. For example, if a player rolls 5,2,4,3,7, and 4, then the following two-digit numbers could be formed:

  23,45,47          42,43,57          43,52,74          44,53,72

- The student then writes the ordered numerals in the third column of the recording sheet.

## Variations of this game:

- Include rules such as "one of the numbers has to be prime," or "all numbers have to be even," etc.

- Set a time limit in which students have to make as many solutions as possible.

- Increase the level of difficulty by making and ordering six-digit numerals.

# Order It to Go!

| | Dice | Write 3 Different Numerals Here | Order Your Numerals Here |
|---|---|---|---|
| Example: | 5 / 4 / 6 / 2 / 3 / 1 | 54 / 62 / 31 | 31 / 54 / 62 |
| 1. | __ / __ / __ / __ / __ / __ | ___ / ___ / ___ | ___ / ___ / ___ |
| 2. | __ / __ / __ / __ / __ / __ | ___ / ___ / ___ | ___ / ___ / ___ |
| 3. | __ / __ / __ / __ / __ / __ | ___ / ___ / ___ | ___ / ___ / ___ |
| 4. | __ / __ / __ / __ / __ / __ | ___ / ___ / ___ | ___ / ___ / ___ |
| 5. | __ / __ / __ / __ / __ / __ | ___ / ___ / ___ | ___ / ___ / ___ |
| 6. | __ / __ / __ / __ / __ / __ | ___ / ___ / ___ | ___ / ___ / ___ |
| 7. | __ / __ / __ / __ / __ / __ | ___ / ___ / ___ | ___ / ___ / ___ |
| 8. | __ / __ / __ / __ / __ / __ | ___ / ___ / ___ | ___ / ___ / ___ |
| 9. | __ / __ / __ / __ / __ / __ | ___ / ___ / ___ | ___ / ___ / ___ |
| 10. | __ / __ / __ / __ / __ / __ | ___ / ___ / ___ | ___ / ___ / ___ |
| 11. | __ / __ / __ / __ / __ / __ | ___ / ___ / ___ | ___ / ___ / ___ |
| 12. | __ / __ / __ / __ / __ / __ | ___ / ___ / ___ | ___ / ___ / ___ |

Name _____     Date _____

# Numeration Activities through 100,000,000

# Tile It!

## Preparation:

- Number small tiles from 0-9. These tiles can come from various sources. Commercially made tiles are available from school supplies. Generally, the tiles are 1" squares made from clear plastic. Tile patterns are on page 65. Copy the tiles on index stock paper and laminate. Tiles can also be made from small one-inch bathroom tiles . The numerals can be written on the tiles with permanent markers.

- Select a work mat from pages 74-80. The level is identified at the top of each work mat. The example below is based on page 68.

- Have an overhead work mat and overhead tiles (page 63) available.

## Procedure:

- Distribute a set of tiles (0-9) and the work mat on page 68 to each student.

- Begin by using an overhead transparency of the work mat on page 68. Explain to the students that they will work on one problem at a time. Each work mat may have several problems on it. Point out the six problems on the work mat on page 66.

- Model for the students how to complete the work mat. Show the students that to solve the problems they will need a tile for each number 0-9. A sample dialogue could be the following:

    *First, notice that problem 1A is 549. Look at section A on the mat. We will begin here. What digit in 549 is in the ones place? (9). Nine is correct. Place your 9-tile on the ones place block. What number is in the tens place in 549? (4). Four is correct. Place your 4-tile in the tens place block. What digit in 549 is in the hundreds place? (5). Five is correct. Place your 5-tile in the hundreds place block. You have finished problem 1A. Do not remove your tiles from section A.*

    *Now look at section B. you are going to do problem 1B in this area. What number is in the hundreds place in the number 632? (6). Six is correct. Place your 6-tile in section B on the hundreds place block. What number is in the ones place? (2). Two is correct. Place your 2-tile in the ones place block. What number is in the tens place? (3). Three is*

*correct. Place your 3-tile in the tens place block. You have just completed problem 1B.*
*Do not remove your tiles. Complete 1C in the same manner.*

- When the students have finished with problems 1Z, 1B, and 1C, they should discover that they have used all of their tiles only one time, and they should have one tile left. On other work mats there may be more than 1 tile left. Instruct the students to ALWAYS read the hint on each work mat.

- Remember, students should never use a tile twice. As the student's complete problems, remind them to signal for you to come and check their work before they remove the tiles. Answer sheets are available beginning on pages 139. To speed up the checking process, the answer sheets can be given to the students for self-assessment. The students can also use the answer sheets to assist in checking other students' work.

- Blank work mats are found on some of the pages. These may be used by students to design their own **Tile It!** problems.

- **Special note**: On the work mats, the place value blocks are NOT in the order that the students would find them on a Place Value Chart. The blocks on the work mats are, therefore, place vertically to avoid this confusion. The work mats have been designed to allow the students, by looking at the numeral, to distinguish which numerals occupy specific place value positions.

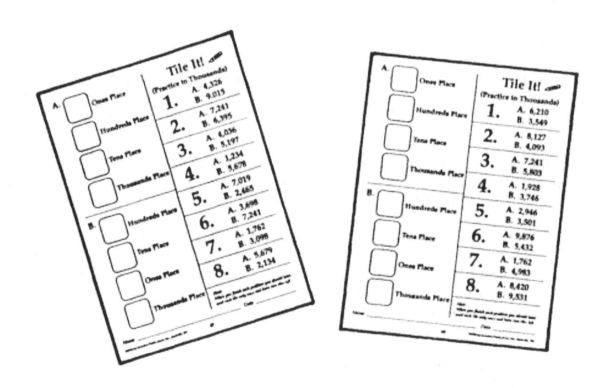

# Overhead Numeral Tiles

| | | | |
|---|---|---|---|
| 0 | 1 | 2 | 3 |
| 4 | 5 | 6 | 7 |
| 8 | 9 | 0 | 0 |
| 0 | 1 | 2 | 3 |
| 4 | 5 | 6 | 7 |
| 8 | 9 | 0 | 0 |

## A.

□ Ones Place

□ Tens Place

□ Hundreds Place

## B.

□ Hundreds Place

□ Ones Place

□ Tens Place

## C.

□ Tens Place

□ Hundreds Place

□ Ones Place

Name _____

# Tile It! ✎
## (Practice to Hundreds)

**1.**
A. 549
B. 632
C. 817

**2.**
A. 165
B. 439
C. 872

**3.**
A. 452
B. 603
C. 791

**4.**
A. 207
B. 549
C. 136

**5.**
A. 327
B. 459
C. 106

**6.**
A. 891
B. 327
C. 450

*Hint:*
*When you finish each problem you should have used each tile only once and have one tile left.*

Date _____

**A.**

☐ Ones Place

☐ Tens Place

☐ Hundreds Place

**B.**

☐ Hundreds Place

☐ Ones Place

☐ Tens Place

**C.**

☐ Tens Place

☐ Hundreds Place

☐ Ones Place

# Tile It! ✏

## (Practice to Hundreds)

**1.**
A. 261
B. 483
C. 579

**2.**
A. 385
B. 467
C. 201

**3.**
A. 273
B. 804
C. 519

**4.**
A. 902
B. 375
C. 648

**5.**
A. 372
B. 416
C. 895

**6.**
A. 721
B. 403
C. 586

*Hint:*
*When you finish each problem you should have used each tile only once and have one tile left.*

Name _____  Date _____

## A.

☐ Ones Place

☐ Tens Place

☐ Hundreds Place

## B.

☐ Hundreds Place

☐ Ones Place

☐ Tens Place

## C.

☐ Tens Place

☐ Hundreds Place

☐ Ones Place

# Tile It! ✎

## (Practice to Hundreds)

Design a **Tile It!** work mat for a friend. Remember, use each numeral tile only once. When solved, your friend should have one tile left in each problem.

**1.**  A. _____
B. _____
C. _____

**2.**  A. _____
B. _____
C. _____

**3.**  A. _____
B. _____
C. _____

**4.**  A. _____
B. _____
C. _____

**5.**  A. _____
B. _____
C. _____

**6.**  A. _____
B. _____
C. _____

Name _____    Date _____

**A.** [ ] Ones Place

[ ] Hundreds Place

[ ] Tens Place

[ ] Thousands Place

**B.** [ ] Hundreds Place

[ ] Tens Place

[ ] Ones Place

[ ] Thousands Place

# Tile It!
## (Practice to Thousands)

| | |
|---|---|
| **1.** | A. 4,326 |
| | B. 9,015 |
| **2.** | A. 7,241 |
| | B. 6,395 |
| **3.** | A. 4,036 |
| | B. 5,197 |
| **4.** | A. 1,234 |
| | B. 5,678 |
| **5.** | A. 7,019 |
| | B. 2,465 |
| **6.** | A. 3,698 |
| | B. 7,241 |
| **7.** | A. 1,762 |
| | B. 3,098 |
| **8.** | A. 5,679 |
| | B. 2,134 |

*Hint:*
*When you finish each problem you should have*
*used each tile only once and have two tiles left.*

Name _____     Date _____

**A.**

☐ Ones Place

☐ Hundreds Place

☐ Tens Place

☐ Thousands Place

**B.**

☐ Hundreds Place

☐ Tens Place

☐ Ones Place

☐ Thousands Place

# Tile It! ✏️

## (Practice to Thousands)

**1.**   A. 6,210
         B. 3,549

**2.**   A. 8,127
         B. 4,093

**3.**   A. 7,241
         B. 5,803

**4.**   A. 1,928
         B. 3,746

**5.**   A. 2,946
         B. 3,501

**6.**   A. 9,876
         B. 5,432

**7.**   A. 1,762
         B. 4,983

**8.**   A. 8,420
         B. 9,531

Hint:
When you finish each problem you should have
used each tile only once and have two tiles left.

Name _____    Date _____

**A.**

☐ **Ones Place**

☐ **Hundreds Place**

☐ **Tens Place**

☐ **Thousands Place**

**B.**

☐ **Hundreds Place**

☐ **Tens Place**

☐ **Ones Place**

☐ **Thousands Place**

# Tile It! ✏

## (Practice to Thousands)

Design a **Tile It!** work mat for a friend. Remember, use each numeral tile only once. When solved, your friend should have two tiles left in each problem.

**1.**  A. _____
    B. _____

**2.**  A. _____
    B. _____

**3.**  A. _____
    B. _____

**4.**  A. _____
    B. _____

**5.**  A. _____
    B. _____

**6.**  A. _____
    B. _____

**7.**  A. _____
    B. _____

**8.**  A. _____
    B. _____

Name _____  Date _____

| | | |
|---|---|---|
| ☐ | **Tens Place** | |
| ☐ | **Ten Thousands Place** | |
| ☐ | **Hundreds Place** | |
| ☐ | **Thousands Place** | |
| ☐ | **Ones Place** | |
| ☐ | **Hundred Thousands Place** | |

# Tile It! ✏

## (Practice to Hundred Thousands)

**1.** 432,569

**2.** 163,428

**3.** 431,265

**4.** 501,263

**5.** 472,135

**6.** 962,157

**7.** 123,456

**8.** 601,795

*Hint:*
*When you finish each problem you should have used each tile only once and have four tiles left.*

Name _____ Date _____

| | | |
|---|---|---|
| ☐ Tens Place | **Tile It!** ✏️ | |
| | **(Practice to Hundred Thousands)** | |
| ☐ Ten Thousands Place | **1.** 107,463 | |
| | **2.** 369,248 | |
| ☐ Hundreds Place | **3.** 135,790 | |
| | **4.** 632,754 | |
| ☐ Thousands Place | **5.** 501,247 | |
| | **6.** 914,265 | |
| ☐ Ones Place | **7.** 403,579 | |
| ☐ Hundred Thousands Place | **8.** 986,012 | |

*Hint:*
*When you finish each problem you should have used each tile only once and have four tiles left.*

Name _____ Date _____

| | |
|---|---|
| ☐ **Tens Place** | # Tile It! ✏ |
| | ## (Practice to Hundred Thousands) |
| ☐ **Ten Thousands Place** | Design a **Tile It!** work mat for a friend. Remember, use each numeral tile only once. When solved, your friend should have four tiles left in each problem. |
| | **1.** _____ |
| ☐ **Hundreds Place** | **2.** _____ |
| | **3.** _____ |
| ☐ **Thousands Place** | **4.** _____ |
| | **5.** _____ |
| ☐ **Ones Place** | **6.** _____ |
| | **7.** _____ |
| ☐ **Hundred Thousands Place** | **8.** _____ |

*Name* _____  *Date* _____

Hundreds Place

Ones Place

Hundred Thousands Place

Tens Place

Thousands Place

Millions Place

Ten Thousands Place

# Tile It!

(Practice to Millions)

**1.** 4,361,205

**2.** 5,073,461

**3.** 2,194,053

**4.** 6,421,930

**5.** 9,308,271

**6.** 7,256,319

**7.** 1,245,968

**8.** 3,962,071

*Hint:*
*When you finish each problem you should have used each tile only once and have three tiles left.*

Name _____ Date _____

| | |
|---|---|
| Hundreds Place | # Tile It! ✎ <br> **(Practice to Millions)** |
| | **1.** 1,234,567 |
| Ones Place | **2.** 2,139,648 |
| Hundred Thousands Place | **3.** 9,876,543 |
| | **4.** 1,073,542 |
| Tens Place | **5.** 2,468,035 |
| | **6.** 9,128,347 |
| Thousands Place | **7.** 5,730,281 |
| Millions Place | **8.** 1,357,924 |
| Ten Thousands Place | *Hint:* <br> *When you finish each problem you should have used each tile only once and have three tiles left.* |

☐ **Hundreds Place**

☐ **Ones Place**

☐ **Hundred Thousands Place**

☐ **Tens Place**

☐ **Thousands Place**

☐ **Millions Place**

☐ **Ten Thousands Place**

# Tile It! ✏️

## (Practice to Millions)

Design a **Tile It!** work mat for a friend. Remember, use each numeral tile only once. When solved, your friend should have three tiles left in each problem.

**1.** _____

**2.** _____

**3.** _____

**4.** _____

**5.** _____

**6.** _____

**7.** _____

**8.** _____

Name _____     Date _____

| | |
|---|---|
| ☐ Tens Place | |
| ☐ Hundred Thousands Place | |
| ☐ Ten Thousands Place | |
| ☐ Millions Place | |
| ☐ Ones Place | |
| ☐ Hundred Millions Place | |
| ☐ Thousands Place | |
| ☐ Hundreds Place | |
| ☐ Ten Millions Place | |

# Tile It! ✏

### (Practice to Hundred Millions)

**1.** 567,432,189

**2.** 730,126,594

**3.** 371,065,429

**4.** 705,318,246

**5.** 123,456,789

Hint:
*When you finish each problem you should have used each tile only once and have one tile left.*

Name _____ Date _____

| | |
|---|---|
| ☐ Tens Place | # Tile It! ✏️ |
| | **(Practice to Hundred Millions)** |
| ☐ Hundred Thousands Place | **1.** 192,837,465 |
| ☐ Ten Thousands Place | |
| ☐ Millions Place | **2.** 369,248,017 |
| ☐ Ones Place | **3.** 593,276,104 |
| ☐ Hundred Millions Place | **4.** 987,654,321 |
| ☐ Thousands Place | |
| ☐ Hundreds Place | **5.** 721,654,980 |
| ☐ Ten Millions Place | *Hint:* *When you finish each problem you should have used each tile only once and have one tile left.* |

Name _____  Date _____

| | |
|---|---|
| ☐ Tens Place | # Tile It! ✏️ |
| ☐ Hundred Thousands Place | ## (Practice to Hundred Millions) |
| ☐ Ten Thousands Place | Design a **Tile It!** work mat for a friend. Remember, use each numeral tile only once. When solved, your friend should have one tile left in each problem. |
| ☐ Millions Place | **1.** _____ |
| ☐ Ones Place | **2.** _____ |
| ☐ Hundred Millions Place | **3.** _____ |
| ☐ Thousands Place | **4.** _____ |
| ☐ Hundreds Place | |
| ☐ Ten Millions Place | **5.** _____ |

Name _____    Date _____

*Writing numerals through hundred millions*

# Word Names Tiles It!

## Preparation:

• Numeral tiles (page 61) & Overhead tiles (page 63)

• Select a work mat from pages 82-90

• Overhead projector & Overhead transparency of page 82

## Procedure:

• Make the 0-9 tiles (page 61)

• Begin by using an overhead transparency of the work mat on page 82. Explain to the students that they will work on one problem at a time. Each work mat may have several problems on it. Point out that the work mat on page 82 has five problems on it altogether. A sample dialogue could be the following:

> *Problem 1A is one hundred ninety-three. I will read the number to myself and place the tiles in the blocks as I say the words. I will place the numeral 1 in the first block, beside the A. The 1 represents 100. In the second block I will place the 9 tile. The tile represents 9 tens or 90. In the third block I will place a 3. The 3 represents 3 ones. I am not to remove my tiles at this time.*

> *Now it's time to do 1B. The number is six hundred twenty-five. I will place the 6 in the first block, beside the B. This tile represents 6 hundreds. In the second block I will place a 2. This tile will represent 2 tens or 20. In the third block I will place a 5. The 5 represents 5 ones. I am still not to remove my tiles at this time.*

> *Now it's time to do 1C. The number is four hundred seventy-eight. I will place the numeral 4 in the first block, beside the C. The 4 tile represents 4 hundreds or 400. In the second block I will place a 7. This tile represents 7 tens or 70. In the third block I will place an 8. The 8 represents 8 ones. I am still not to remove my tiles until my work is checked.*

> *I will read the hint: "You should use each tile only once and have one tile left." Let's see. I have used all my tiles one time, and I have the 0 tile left. I think I have done it correctly.*

• Remember, each problem never uses a tile twice. As the students complete problems, remind them to signal you to come check their work before they remove the tiles. Answer sheets are available beginning on page 139. To speed up the checking process, the answer sheets can be given to the students for self-assessment. You can also use students who finish first to check other students' work with an answer sheet. Blank work mats are found on pages 84,86,88, and 90. These could be used by students to design their own **Word Names Tile It!** problems.

# Word Names Tile It!

## (Practice to Hundreds)

A. ☐ ☐ ☐

B. ☐ ☐ ☐

C. ☐ ☐ ☐

**1.**
A. one hundred ninety-three
B. six hundred twenty-five
C. four hundred seventy-eight

**2.**
A. six hundred twenty-one
B. ninety-five
C. three hundred forty-seven

**3.**
A. two hundred four
B. one hundred thirty-seven
C. six hundred fifty-nine

**4.**
A. four hundred ninety-six
B. one hundred twenty-three
C. five hundred eight

**5.**
A. seven hundred thirty
B. one hundred fifty-six
C. two hundred forty-eight

*Hint: You should use each tile once and have one tile left.*

Name _____ Date _____

# Word Names Tile It!

## (Practice to Hundreds)

A. ☐ ☐ ☐

B. ☐ ☐ ☐

C. ☐ ☐ ☐

**1.**
A. Five hundred sixty-two
B. One hundred four
C. Nine hundred eighty-seven

**2.**
A. Four hundred thirty-two
B. One hundred five
C. Nine hundred sixty-seven

**3.**
A. Nine hundred six
B. Five hundred thirty-one
C. Seven hundred twenty-four

**4.**
A. Fifty-four
B. Three hundred twenty-nine
C. One hundred sixty-eight

**5.**
A. Seventeen
B. Eight hundred forty-six
C. Nine hundred twenty-three

*Hint: You should use each tile only once and have one tile left.*

Name _____ Date _____

# Word Names Tile It!

## (Practice to Hundreds)

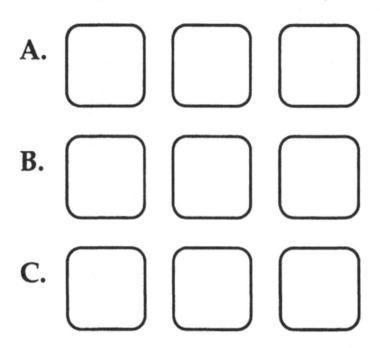

A.  ☐ ☐ ☐

B.  ☐ ☐ ☐

C.  ☐ ☐ ☐

Design a **Word Names Tile It!** work mat for a friend. Remember, use each numeral tile only
once. When solved, your friend should have one tile left.

**1.**  A. _____
    B. _____
    C. _____

**2.**  A. _____
    B. _____
    C. _____

**3.**  A. _____
    B. _____
    C. _____

Name _____ Date _____

# Word Names Tile It!

## (Practice to Thousands)

A. ☐ , ☐ ☐ ☐

B. ☐ , ☐ ☐ ☐

**1.** A. One thousand, four hundred ninety-two
B. Three thousand, eight hundred sixty-seven

**2.** A. Six thousand, seven hundred thirty-two
B. Five thousand, four hundred one

**3.** A. Nine thousand forty-three
B. Two thousand, one hundred fifty-seven

**4.** A. Seven thousand, six hundred twenty-four
B. Five thousand, three hundred ten

**5.** A. Four thousand, three hundred ten
B. Seven thousand, two hundred fifty-nine

**6.** A. Two thousand, fifteen
B. Three thousand, seven hundred forty-nine

*Hint: You should use each tile only once and have two tiles left after each problem.*

Name _____  Date _____

# Word Names Tile It!

## (Practice to Thousands)

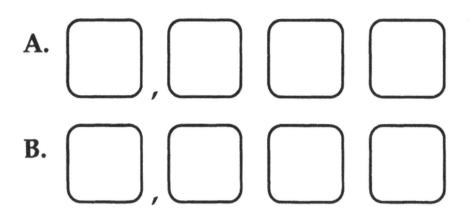

A. ▢ , ▢ ▢ ▢

B. ▢ , ▢ ▢ ▢

**Design a Word Names Tile It!** work mat for a friend. Remember, use each numeral tile only once. When solved, your friend should have two tiles left.

**1.**   A. _____
         B. _____

**2.**   A. _____
         B. _____

**3.**   A. _____
         B. _____

**4.**   A. _____
         B. _____

Name _____   Date _____

# Word Names Tile It!

## (Practice to Hundred Thousands)

[ ][ ][ ],[ ][ ][ ]

**1.** Four hundred fifty-nine thousand, two hundred seventy

**2.** Five hundred twenty-three thousand, four hundred sixty

**3.** Nine hundred forty-eight thousand, three hundred twenty-one

**4.** Eight hundred fifty-four thousand, six hundred seven

**5.** Three hundred twenty thousand, five hundred forty-nine

**6.** Two hundred five thousand, eight hundred sixty-seven

**7.** One hundred fifty-three thousand, four hundred ninety-six

**8.** Seven hundred ninety-two thousand, five hundred one

**9.** Six hundred forty thousand, thirteen

**10.** Three hundred twenty thousand, six hundred fifteen

*Hint: You should use each tile only once and have four tiles left after each problem.*

Name _____    Date _____

# Word Names Tile It!

## (Practice to Hundred Thousands)

Design a **Word Names Tile It!** work mat for a friend. Remember, use each numeral tile only once. When solved, your friend should have four tiles left.

**1.** _____

**2.** _____

**3.** _____

**4.** _____

**5.** _____

Name _____ Date _____

# Word Names Tile It!

## (Practice to Hundred Millions)

[ ] [ ] [ ] , [ ] [ ] [ ] , [ ] [ ] [ ]

**1.** Four hundred five million, two hundred ninety-three thousand, eight hundred seventy-one

**2.** Eight hundred ninety-seven million, six hundred fifty-three thousand, twelve

**3.** Six hundred nine million, three hundred forty-one thousand, five hundred seventy-eight

**4.** Twenty-nine million, eight hundred seventy-five thousand, one hundred forty-six

**5.** Seven hundred thirty-two million, sixty-four thousand, five hundred eighteen

*Hint: You should use each tile only once and have one tile left after each problem.*

Name _____ Date _____

# Word Names Tile It!

## (Practice to Hundred Millions)

[ ][ ][ ],[ ][ ][ ],[ ][ ][ ]

Design a **Word Names Tile It!** work mat for a friend. Remember, use each numeral tile only once. When solved, your friend should have four tiles left.

**1.** _____

**2.** _____

**3.** _____

**4.** _____

**5.** _____

Name _____ Date _____

# NUMERATION CONCEPT:
## *Ordering numbers through thousands*

# Dice Rollers

## Preparation:

- You will need six dice per group. Standard dice can be used for set A, while the other sets can be created using blank wooden dice written on with a marker.

| Set | Number to write on dice |
|-----|-------------------------|
| A   | 1,2,3,4,5,6             |
| B   | 4,5,6,7,8,9             |
| C   | 1,2,3,5,6,7             |
| D   | 0,2,4,5,7,9             |

Easy version of this activity – Use die from sets A,B or A,B,C for each group.
Intermediate version of this activity – Use die from sets A,A,A,B
Advanced version of this activity – Use die from sets A,B,C,D,D

## Procedure:

- Determine the game level appropriate for your students.

- Once student rolls all six dice at one time.

- The student then records on the group's Dice Rollers recording sheet (see page 92) the resulting six numbers in one of the rectangles in the "Dice Thrown" column. The student records the largest possible numeral that can be created using the dice that were rolled. The student records the smallest possible numeral that can be created using the dice that were rolled.

- The next student in the group follows the same procedure, until each student has had at least one turn.

# Dice Rollers

| | Dice Thrown | Largest Number Possible | Smallest Number Possible |
|---|---|---|---|
| 1. | | | |
| 2. | | | |
| 3. | | | |
| 4. | | | |
| 5. | | | |
| 6. | | | |
| 7. | | | |
| 8. | | | |
| 9. | | | |
| 10. | | | |

Name _____ Date _____

## NUMERATION CONCEPT:
### *Representing money*

# Money Changers

## Preparation:

- Create a bank of play money. Patters for play money are on pages 94-97. Prepare at least 100 ones, 100 fives, 100 tens, 100 twenties, 100 fifties, 100 hundreds, and 10 thousands.

- Create a divided tray (till) for the play money.

## Procedure:

- Allow one student to assume the role of the banker. The student stands in front of the "bank."

- Begin by telling the class that you need to change for your $100 bill. Inform the students how many of the bills are in the bank. Could the banker change the $200 bill using only fifties? (Yes). How many fifties would the banker give for a $100 bill? (2). Hand the banker the #100 bill. The banker should give two fifties back. Ask the students if the banker could exchange the two fifties for $10 bills. Permit a student to tell the banker how many tens he or she should give back. Continue in this manner to give the students a variety of opportunities to exchange the money.

- Choose a student to come to the bank and select a sum of money. This student counts the money and informs the class how much he or she has altogether. The student then calls on other students to tell how that amount of money could be exchanged.

- This activity can become a banking center in the classroom. Have various amounts of money written on index cards. Let one student draw a card and count out that amount of money. Another student changes the money into different denominations of bills.

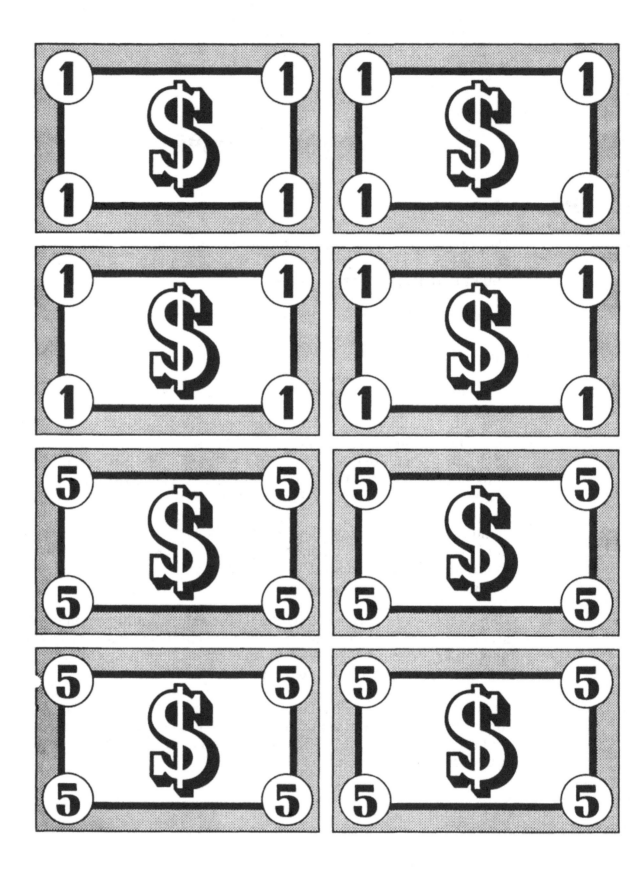

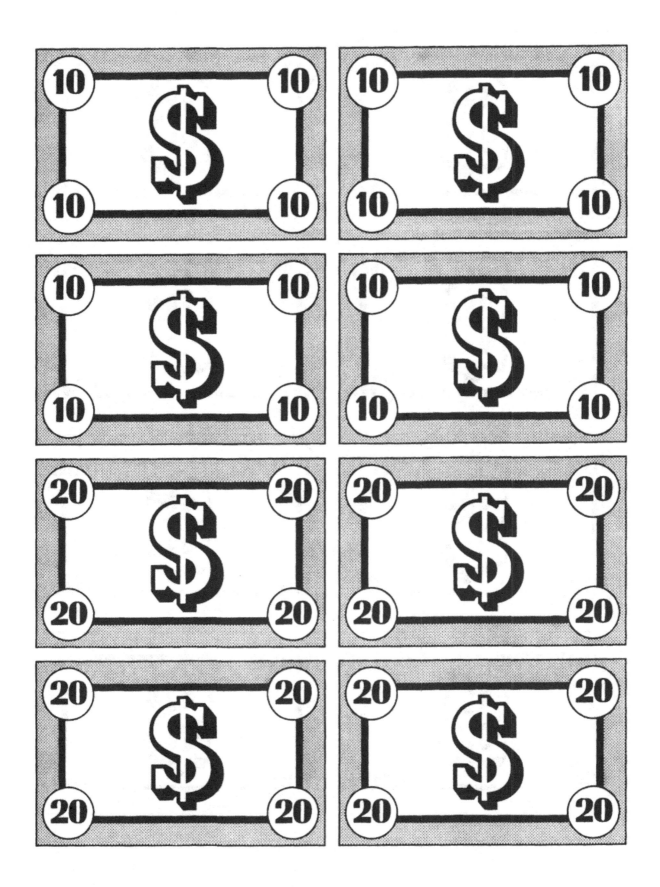

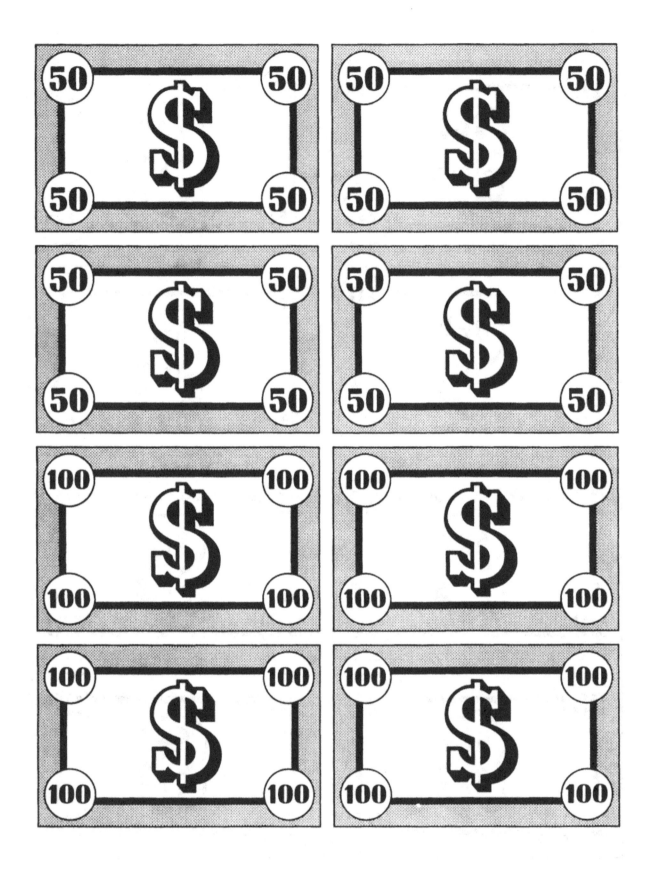

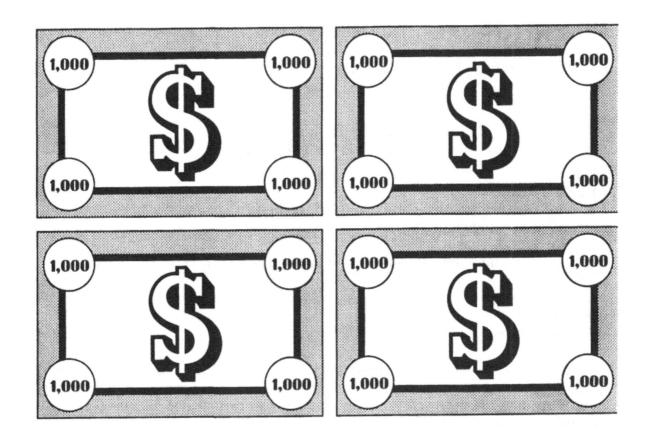

# NUMERATION CONCEPT:
## *Identifying place value*

# Tile a Value!

## Preparation:
- Numeral tiles (instructions on page 61); Overhead transparency of page 99 and overhead tiles (page 63)

- Select a work mat from pages 99-106. The level is identified at the top of each work mat.

## Procedure:
- Distribute 0-9 tiles sets.

- Begin by using an overhead transparency of the work mat on page 99. Explain to the students that they will work on one problem at a time. Each work mat may have several problems on it. Point out that this work mat has four problems altogether. A sample dialogue could be the following:

> *Problem 1A is 4,542. The 4 is underlined. It is in the thousands place. I will place my 4-tile on the block in column A marked **Thousands Place**. In the next numeral (3,219), the 9 is underlined. The 9 is in the ones place. I will place my 9-tile in the block that is labeled **Ones Place** in column A.*
> *The third numeral is 5,630. The 6 is underlined, and it is in the hundreds place. I will place my 6-tile in the block labeled **Hundreds Place** in column A. The last numeral in 1A is 1,482. The 8 is underlined, and it is in the tens place. I will place my 8-tile in the block labeled **Tens Place**. I am not to remove my tiles until I complete problem B.*
> *Now it's time to do 1B. I will follow the same procedure as I did in Problem 1A. (The teacher continues in the same fashion as in problem 2A).*

- Remember, each problem never uses the same tile twice. Instruct the students to read the hint on each work mat to determine the number of tiles left after the problem is completed.

- As the students complete their problems, remind them to signal for you to come and check their work before they remove the tiles. Answer sheets are available on page 143. To speed up the checking process, the answer sheets can be given to the students for self-assessment. The students can also use the answer sheets to assist you in checking other students' work.

- Special Note: On the work mats, the place value blocks are NOT in the order that the students would find them on a Place Value Chart. This is designed to allow the students, by looking at a numeral, to distinguish which numerals occupy specific place value positions.

# Tile a Value!

## (Practice to Thousands)

**A.**

[ ] *Thousands Place* **,000**

[ ] *Hundreds Place* **00**

[ ] *Tens Place* **0**

[ ] *Ones Place*

**B.**

[ ] *Tens Place* **0**

[ ] *Thousands Place* **,000**

[ ] *Ones Place*

[ ] *Hundreds Place* **00**

**1.** A. 4,542
3,219
5,630
1,482

B. 5,431
3,679
2,650
7,321

**2.** A. 5,432
6,591
7,632
4,301

B. 2,695
4,631
5,647
2,451

**3.** A. 3,269
4,013
2,154
1,348

B. 9,568
2,456
5,621
7,369

**4.** A. 4,629
5,468
3,201
6,987

B. 9,871
4,248
7,653
5,450

Hint: You should use each tile only one time and have two tiles left.

# Tile a Value! ✏️

## (Practice to Thousands)

**A.**

☐ *Thousands Place*
**,000**

☐ *Hundreds Place*
**00**

☐ *Tens Place*
**0**

☐ *Ones Place*

**B.**

☐ *Tens Place*
**0**

☐ *Thousands Place*
**,000**

☐ *Ones Place*

☐ *Hundreds Place*
**00**

Design a **Tile a Value!** work mat for a friend. Remember, use each numeral tile only once. When solved, your friend should have two tiles left.

**A.** _____

_____

_____

_____

**B.** _____

_____

_____

_____

*Name* _____ *Date* _____

# Tile a Value!

## (Practice to Hundred Thousands)

Hundreds Place
**00**

Ones Place

Thousands Place
**,000**

Hundred
Thousands Place
**00,000**

Ten Thousands
Place
**0,000**

Tens Place
**0**

A.  1.    5,<u>4</u>13

   2.    <u>9</u>,462

   3. 342,98<u>6</u>

   4. 562,4<u>3</u>0

   5. <u>7</u>56,985

   6. 5<u>8</u>3,207

B.  1. 5<u>6</u>9,410

   2. 362,<u>5</u>84

   3. <u>1</u>23,547

   4. 569,<u>3</u>21

   5. 105,4<u>7</u>3

   6. 289,65<u>4</u>

Hint: You should use each tile only one time and have four tiles left.

# Tile a Value! ✎

## (Practice to Hundred Thousands)

☐ **Hundreds Place**
**00**

☐ **Ones Place**

☐ **Thousands Place**
**,000**

☐ **Hundred Thousands Place**
**00,000**

☐ **Ten Thousands Place**
**0,000**

☐ **Tens Place**
**0**

Design a Tile a Value! work mat for a friend. Remember, use each numeral tile only once. When solved, your friend should have four tiles left.

**A.** 1. _____

2. _____

3. _____

4. _____

5. _____

6. _____

**B.** 1. _____

2. _____

3. _____

4. _____

5. _____

6. _____

Name _____ Date _____

# Tile a Value!

## (Practice to Millions)

Hundred Thousands Place
**00,000**

Thousands Place
**,000**

Tens Place
**0**

Ten Thousands Place
**0,000**

Hundreds Place
**00**

Ones Place

Millions Place
**,000,000**

**A.**
1. 3,291,622
2. 2,687,321
3. 3,210,948
4. 9,365,430
5. 5,436,987
6. 2,653,333
7. 4,609,437

**B.**
1. 1,546,327
2. 3,654,221
3. 7,269,832
4. 5,674,328
5. 4,691,765
6. 9,863,104
7. 2,386,521

Hint: You should use each tile only one time and have three tiles left.

# Tile a Value! ✏️

## (Practice to Millions)

☐ **Hundred Thousands Place**
**00,000**

☐ **Thousands Place**
**,000**

☐ **Tens Place**
**0**

☐ **Ten Thousands Place**
**0,000**

☐ **Hundreds Place**
**00**

☐ **Ones Place**

☐ **Millions Place**
**,000,000**

Design a **Tile a Value!** work mat for a friend. Remember, use each numeral tile only once. When solved, your friend should have three tiles left.

A.
1. _____
2. _____
3. _____
4. _____
5. _____
6. _____
7. _____

B.
1. _____
2. _____
3. _____
4. _____
5. _____
6. _____
7. _____

Name _____ Date _____

# Tile a Value!

## (Practice to Hundred Millions)

| | |
|---|---|
| ☐ **Thousands Place** ,000 | ☐ **Ones Place** |
| ☐ **Hundreds Place** 00 | ☐ **Tens Place** 0 |
| ☐ **Ten Thousands Place** 0,000 | ☐ **Hundred Millions Place** 00,000,000 |
| ☐ **Hundred Thousands Place** 00,000 | ☐ **Millions Place** ,000,000 |
| ☐ **Ten Millions Place** 0,000,000 | Hint! You should use each tile only one time and have no tiles left. |

1. 5,017
2. 75,269
3. 604,321

4. 834,629,001
5. 4,732
6. 943,652,075

7. 2,534,691
8. 45,762,801
9. 36,675,409

Name _____     Date _____

# Tile a Value!

## (Practice to Hundred Millions)

*Thousands Place*
**,000**

*Ones Place*

*Hundreds Place*
**00**

*Tens Place*
**0**

*Ten Thousands Place*
**0,000**

*Hundred Millions Place*
**00,000,000**

*Hundred Thousands Place*
**00,000**

*Millions Place*
**,000,000**

*Ten Millions Place*
**0,000,000**

Design a **Tile a Value!** work mat for a friend. Remember, use each numeral tile only once. When solved, your friend should have no tiles left.

1. _____    4. _____    7. _____
2. _____    5. _____    8. _____
3. _____    6. _____    9. _____

Name _____    Date _____

# Those Large Numbers

## Preparation:

- Create the chart below so that the class can see:

| Billions Period | Millions Period | Thousands Period | Ones Period |
|---|---|---|---|
|  |  |  |  |

## Procedure:

- Ask four students to come to the chart. Each student is assigned to one of the place value periods on the chart.

- Each student is to write three numerals in his or her section of the chart, with the exception of the student assigned to the billions period.

  The student assigned to the billions section may write one, two, or three numerals.

- Another student in the class is asked to read the entire number. If the student reads the number correctly, the student may trade places with a student at the chart.

- For a variation of this game for younger students, create a chart with ones, tens and hundreds periods.

# Numeration Activities through 100,000,000,000

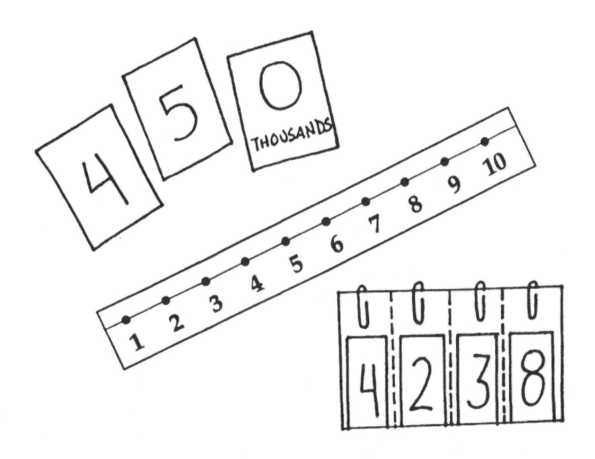

# NUMERATION CONCEPT:
## *Identifying numbers through the billions period*

# Line Up!

## Preparation:

• Make two sets of large cards with the numerals 0-9 on them. In each set include three additional zeros. At the bottom of the cards with the zeros, write the period that the additional zeros will be used in: thousands, millions, or billions.

• Make three cards with large commas on them.

## Procedure:

• Separate the class into two teams of fifteen students each. Additional students can be scorekeepers or checkers. Have one team line up in the front of the classroom and the other team line up in the back of the classroom.

• Pass the cards to each team.

• Call out a large number and say, "Go!"

• At that point the teams form the number that you called out. The first team to form the number correctly scores a point.

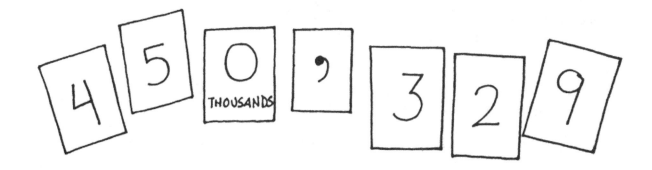

# Expanding the Numerals

## Preparation:

• Make a Place Value Displayer

• Create several sets of numeral cards

## To make a Place Value Displayer

• A 24" x 10" strip of construction paper

• Twenty 8" x 1 ½ " tag board strips

• Paper clips

• Markers

Fold the 24" x 10" strip of construction paper in accordion folds. Ten folds are necessary to create a Place Value Displayer that will show up to the thousands place (see the diagram on page 113).

Fold the bottom edge of the 24" x 10" strip of construction paper up about 2 inches to create a pocket. This pocket will serve as a holder for the numeral cards. Staple this fold as shown in the diagram below.

Use a marker to label the place value positions and the addition signs as shown in the diagram below.

The twenty 8" x 1 ½" tag board strips will be used to create sets of numeral cards. Label the strips with the numerals 0-9. Two sets would allow for more combinations of numerals. These strips can be inserted into the displayer to show various numerals.

## Procedure:

- Insert numeral cards into the displayer to show 4,238. Fold and clip the displayer as shown in the diagram below. When the displayer is folded and clipped, students can see on the standard numeral.

- Ask the students how many ones are in the number 4,238. As they respond, unclip the ones place on the displayer. This will verify their response. Continue asking the students place value questions. Verify their answers by continuing to unclip the Place Value Displayer.

- Allow students to place numerals in the Place Value Displayer. The students can quiz each other on the place value positions of the new numerals.

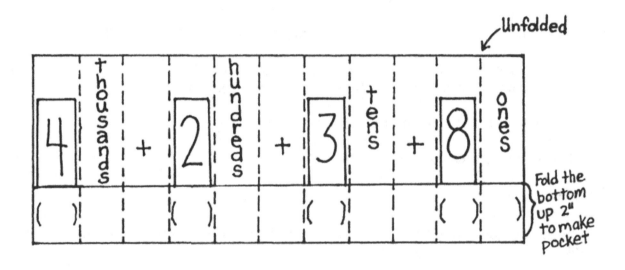

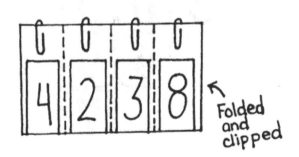

# NUMERATION CONCEPT:
*Showing and reading numerals in expanded form*

# Expansion

## Preparation:

- One sheet of graph paper with one-inch squares for each student (page 116).

- One sheet of graph paper with one-centimeter squares for each student (page 117).

- A set of 0-9 tiles and two additional 0 tiles for each student (page 63-65).

- An overhead transparency of page 117 and an over transparency of 0-9 tiles with two additional tiles. Cut these to create the tiles (page 65).

- Overhead transparency markers

- Play money (pages 94-97).

## Procedure:

- On the top margin of the overhead transparency of page 116, write the numeral 347.

- Place the overhead tiles in the following position:

- Instruct the students that this is a demonstration of 300 + 40 + 7. Write this notation on the overhead. Explain to the students that this form of the number is the expanded form (or expanded notation) of the number.

- Remove the tiles and erase 347. Write the numeral 685 in the top margin of the overhead transparency. Ask the students to move the tiles on their graph paper to demonstrate the expanded form of 685. When the students have had adequate time to complete this task, allow one student to place the correct answer on the overhead. All students can check their answers with the student's demonstration on the overhead.

- Practice this procedure several times until the students fully understand the concept.

- To move the students to a more abstract method of writing expanded form, use the one-centimeter graph paper. Write a numeral on the board, such as 3,472. Ask the students to use the squares on the graph paper to write this number in expanded form. The illustration below shows what the students' work should look like.

| 3 | 0 | 0 | 0 |
|---|---|---|---|
|   | 4 | 0 | 0 |
|   |   | 7 | 0 |
|   |   |   | 2 |

$$3,000 + 400 + 70 + 2 = 3,472$$

- A variation of this activity can be done with play money (See pages 94-97 for sample play money). Select 3 thousand-dollar bills, 4 hundred-dollar bills, 7 ten-dollar bills, and 2 one-dollar bills. Ask the students to write this value of money, in expanded form, on the graph paper.

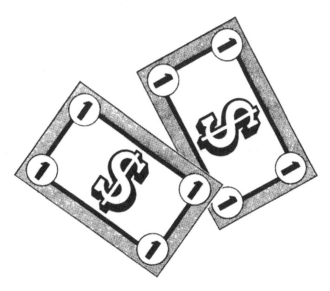

# One-Inch Graph Paper

# One-Centimeter Graph Paper

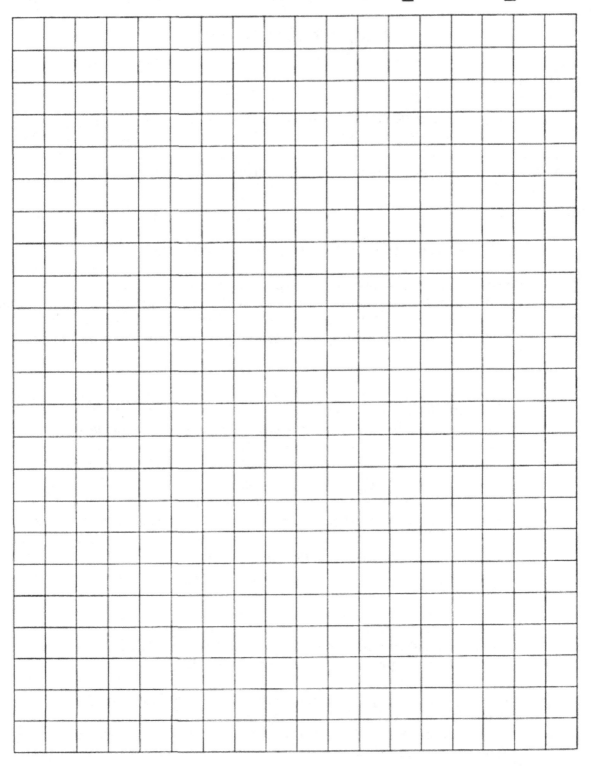

# NUMERATION CONCEPT:
## *Reading numerals in expanded form*

# Expand a Tile!

## Preparation:

- Numeral tiles 0-9 and two additional 0 tiles (page 61).
- Select a work mat from pages 119-126. The level is identified at the top of each work mat.
- Overhead transparency of page 119 and overhead tiles (page 63).

## Procedure:

- Assemble the 0-9 tiles and the two additional 0 tiles.

- Begin by using an overhead transparency of the work mat found on page 119. Explain to the students that they will work on one problem at a time. Each work mat may have several problems on it. Point out that this work mat has four problems altogether. A sample dialogue could be the following:

  *In problem 1, part A is 100 + 2. I will place a 1-tile in the block that could represent the hundreds place. I will place a 0-tile in the tens place and a 2-tile in the ones place. These tiles will remain on the work mat. To complete part B, I will place a 3-tile in the hundreds place, a 4-tile in the tens place, and a 5-tile in the ones place. I will leave all the tiles I have put on my work mat in place. To complete part C, I will place a 9-tile in the hundreds place, an 8-tile in the tens place, and a 7-tile in the ones place. All of these tiles remain on my mat. To complete the puzzle, I will now complete part D. I will put a 6-tile in the hundreds place, a 0-tile in the tens place, and a 0-tile in the ones place. If I have done the **Expand A Tile** exercise correctly, I should have no tiles left. All of my tiles have been used one time and I have no tiles left, so I probably did the exercise correctly.*

- Remember, each problem never uses the same tile twice. Instruct the students to read the hint on each work mat to determine the number of tiles left after the problem has been completed.

- As the student's complete problems, remind them to signal you to come and check their work before they remove their tiles. An answer key is available on page 145. To speed up the checking process, the answer key can be given to the students for self-assessment. The students can also use the answer key to assist you in checking other students' work.

# Expand a Tile!

## (Practice to Hundreds)

A. ☐ ☐ ☐

B. ☐ ☐ ☐

C. ☐ ☐ ☐

D. ☐ ☐ ☐

**1.**
A. 100 + 2
B. 300 + 40 + 5
C. 900 + 80 + 7
D. 600 + 0

**3.**
A. 900 + 60
B. 800 + 3
C. 700 + 50 + 2
D. 40 + 1

**2.**
A. 70 + 5
B. 200 + 90 + 6
C. 400 + 1
D. 300 + 8

**4.**
A. 100 + 7
B. 200 + 50
C. 300 + 8
D. 400 + 60 + 9

*Hint: You should use each tile only once (including the two extra 0 tiles) and have NO tiles left.*

# Expand a Tile!

## (Practice to Hundreds)

A. ☐ ☐ ☐

B. ☐ ☐ ☐

C. ☐ ☐ ☐

D. ☐ ☐ ☐

Design an **Expand a Tile!** work mat for a friend. Remember, use each numeral tile only once (including the two extra 0-tiles). When solved, your friend should have NO tiles left.

**1.**  A. _____

B. _____

C. _____

D. _____

**2.**  A. _____

B. _____

C. _____

D. _____

Name _____ Date _____

# Expand a Tile!

## (Practice to Thousands)

A. ☐ , ☐ ☐ ☐

B. ☐ , ☐ ☐ ☐

C. ☐ , ☐ ☐ ☐

**1.**
A. 5,000 + 200 + 10
B. 4,000 + 300 + 9
C. 7,000 + 600 + 80

**2.**
A. 9,000 + 700 + 3
B. 6,000 + 40 + 2
C. 8,000 + 500 + 1

**3.**
A. 5,000 + 1
B. 2,000 + 300 + 40 + 6
C. 7,000 + 900 + 80

**4.**
A. 3,000 + 20
B. 1,000 + 500 + 90 + 7
C. 6,000 + 40 + 8

**5.**
A. 2,000 + 100 + 9
B. 7,000 + 80 + 5
C. 6,000 + 30 + 4

**6.**
A. 6,000 + 100 + 30 + 9
B. 4,000 + 70
C. 8,000 + 20 + 5

*Hint: You should use each tile only once (including the two extra 0 tiles) and have NO tiles left.*

# Expand a Tile! 🖊️

## (Practice to Thousands)

A. ⬜ , ⬜ ⬜ ⬜

B. ⬜ , ⬜ ⬜ ⬜

C. ⬜ , ⬜ ⬜ ⬜

Design an **Expand a Tile!** work mat for a friend. Remember, use each numeral tile only once (including the two extra 0-tiles). When solved, your friend should have NO tiles left.

**1.**
A. _____
B. _____
C. _____

**2.**
A. _____
B. _____
C. _____

Name _____ Date _____

# Expand a Tile!

## (Practice to Hundred Thousands)

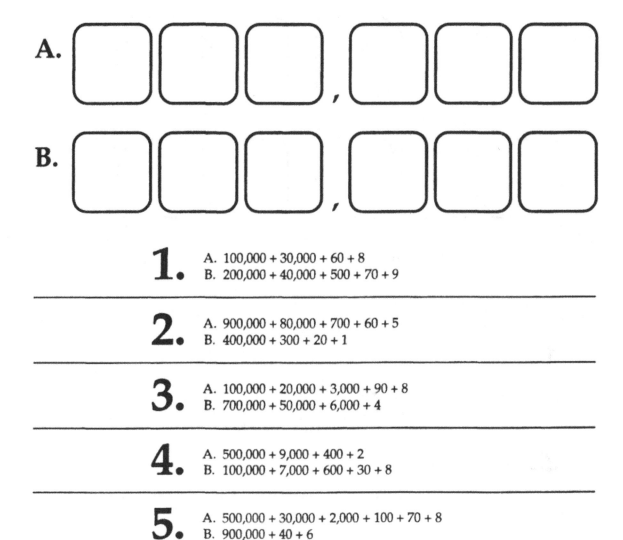

**A.** ⬜⬜⬜,⬜⬜⬜

**B.** ⬜⬜⬜,⬜⬜⬜

**1.**
A. 100,000 + 30,000 + 60 + 8
B. 200,000 + 40,000 + 500 + 70 + 9

**2.**
A. 900,000 + 80,000 + 700 + 60 + 5
B. 400,000 + 300 + 20 + 1

**3.**
A. 100,000 + 20,000 + 3,000 + 90 + 8
B. 700,000 + 50,000 + 6,000 + 4

**4.**
A. 500,000 + 9,000 + 400 + 2
B. 100,000 + 7,000 + 600 + 30 + 8

**5.**
A. 500,000 + 30,000 + 2,000 + 100 + 70 + 8
B. 900,000 + 40 + 6

**6.**
A. 400,000 + 5,000 + 700 + 90
B. 100,000 + 30,000 + 2,000 + 60 + 8

*Hint: You should use each tile only once (including the two extra 0 tiles) and have NO tiles left.*

# Expand a Tile! ✐

## (Practice to Hundred Thousands)

A. ⬜⬜⬜,⬜⬜⬜

B. ⬜⬜⬜,⬜⬜⬜

Design an **Expand a Tile!** work mat for a friend. Remember, use each numeral tile only once (including the two extra 0-tiles). When solved, your friend should have NO tiles left.

**1.** A. _____

B. _____

**2.** A. _____

B. _____

**3.** A. _____

B. _____

Name _____ Date _____

# Expand a Tile! ✐

## (Practice to Millions)

1. 1,000,000 + 500,000 + 40,000 + 6,000 + 700 + 3
2. 9,000,000 + 700,000 + 5,000 + 200 + 10 + 8
3. 1,000,000 + 300,000 + 50,000 + 7,000 + 900 + 20 + 4
4. 3,000,000 + 200,000 + 50,000 + 600 + 90 + 8
5. 4,000,000 + 600,000 + 10 + 2
6. 8,000,000 + 1,000 + 200 + 30 + 4
7. 1,000,000 + 500,000 + 40,000 + 2,000
8. 6,000,000 + 500,000 + 70,000 + 3,000 + 200 + 10
9. 4,000,000 + 90,000 + 5,000 + 800 + 1
10. 1,000,000 + 2,000 + 30 + 4

*Hint: You should use each tile only once and have three tiles left.*

# Expand a Tile! ✐
## (Practice to Millions)

Design an **Expand a Tile!** work mat for a friend. Remember, use each numeral tile only once. When solved, your friend should have **three** tiles left.

1. _____

2. _____

3. _____

4. _____

5. _____

Name _____  Date _____

# NUMERATION CONCEPT:
## *Understanding large numbers*

# How Big is One Million?

## Preparation:

- Gather large containers such as large empty water bottles
- Make a copy of page 128 for each student.

## Procedure:

- Send home the parent letter on page 128. Please fill in the type of object that the students are to bring. The item should be light, small, common, and not a classroom hazard. Popcorn kernels, telephone numbers, different types of cereals, and grains of rice work well. Allow several weeks for the families to accumulate the items.

- It would be wise to make this project a joint effort among several classrooms in the school. If there are 30 students in your class, each student will have to bring over 33,333 items. If they bring the items in bags of 100, that would be over 333 bags! For younger students, make this project adjustable to understand the size of numbers such as 100 or 1,000.

- As the students complete their problems, remind them to signal for you to come and check their work before they remove the tiles. Answer sheets are available on page 143. To speed up the checking process, the answer sheets can be given to the students for self-assessment. The students can also use the answer sheets to assist you in checking other students' work.

- When the items arrive in the classroom, write on the outside of the container(s), "How Big is One Million?" I used large empty water bottles for our collection of popcorn kernels. You will need more than 5! I kept a notebook for students to record our growing collection.

Dear Parent(s) or Guardian(s):

We need your help with a very special math project in our classroom. This project will be a collection of 1 million _____. This is such an enormous project, that we will need as many students in the class to help as possible

Please send _____ bags of 100 _____ to school on _____. Have your student carefully count and fill up each bag. We will add each student's contribution to our collection.

This activity will reinforce many math concepts, including counting, estimating, understanding the size of numbers, and problem solving.

If you have any questions, please feel free to contact me at _____. Thank you so much for your support!

Sincerely,

# NUMERATION CONCEPT:
*Understanding large numbers*

# Have You Ever Seen a Googol?

**Preparation:**
- Roll of adding-machine tape
- markers

**Procedure:**

- Begin discussing large numbers with the students. Ask them to notice any patterns that they see. On the board write the following:

| Word Name | Numeral | Exponential Form |
|---|---|---|
| Thousand | 1,000 | $10^3$ |
| Ten Thousand | 10,000 | $10^4$ |
| Hundred Thousand | 100,000 | $10^5$ |

- Ask the students if they notice a relationship between the number of zeros and the exponent. Ask them to predict what the exponent will be on a million. Ten million? Hundred million? Billion?

| Word Name | Numeral | Exponential Form |
|---|---|---|
| Million | 1,000,000 | $10^5$ |
| Billion | 1,000,000,000 | $10^9$ |
| Trillion | 1,000,000,000,000 | $10^{12}$ |

- At this point the students are looking at the first position in each place value period. What are the students noticing about the exponents between the periods? How much are they increasing?

The next place value periods are the following:

| | |
|---|---|
| Quadrillion | $10^{15}$ |
| Quintrillion | $10^{18}$ |
| Sextillion | $10^{21}$ |
| Septillion | $10^{24}$ |
| Octillion | $10^{27}$ |
| Nonillion | $10^{30}$ |
| Decillion | $10^{33}$ |

- Now, ask the students if they have ever heard of a googol. It is the name for 10 raised to the power of 100. This term was invented in 1938 when Edward

Kasner, a mathematician from the United States, asked his 9-year-old nephew to think up a name for a very large number. In exponential form it is written $10^{100}$. That would be a 1 with 100 zeros!

- The final activity is to ask the students if they would like to make a googol as a class. Ask the students to use their problem-solving strategies to figure out how many zeros each student would have to contribute to make a googol. Have the students write their zeros on the adding machine tape.

- Extension of this activity can be to research Edward Kasner or to determine the value of a googolplex. A googolplex is 10 raised to the power of a googol!

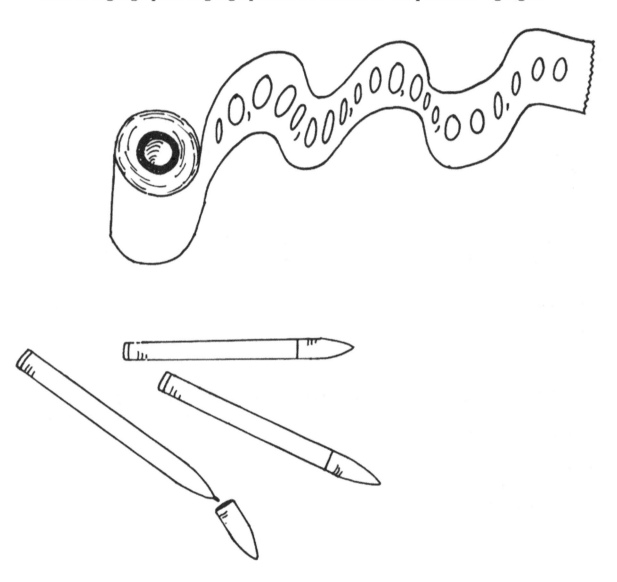

# NUMERATION CONCEPT:
## *Rounding whole numbers to the nearest ten*

# Keeper of the Secret

## Preparation:

- Cut out and tape together a number line for each group of students. Use the patterns on page 132-133. Number lines are also available at school supply stores.

## Procedure:

- Distribute the number lines to the groups of students, and instruct them to place the number lines on their desks in front of their work area.

- Begin by asking the students to look at their number lines and tell the multiple of 10 before and after any particular number. For example, the number 43 has a 40 before it and a 50 after it. Provide lots of practice with this simple activity.

- Begin to teach the students the "keeper of the secret" technique. In 43, the 3 is the "keeper of the secret." The 3 tells you that 43 is closer to 40 than it is to 50. Looking at the number line, the number that is the "keeper of the secret" is below the 5, so it will be rounded down to the last multiple of ten. If the "keeper of the secret" is 5 or above, the number will be rounded up to the next multiple of ten. The 3 in 43 is the "keeper of the secret," and it's below 5, so the number is rounded to 40.

- Continue to call out numbers for the students to round. Have the students write down the numbers. Instruct them to write the multiple of ten before and after the given numbers. Underline the number that is the "keeper of the secret." This method of recording will assist in finding errors in the students work.

# "Keeper of the Secret" Number line (part 1)

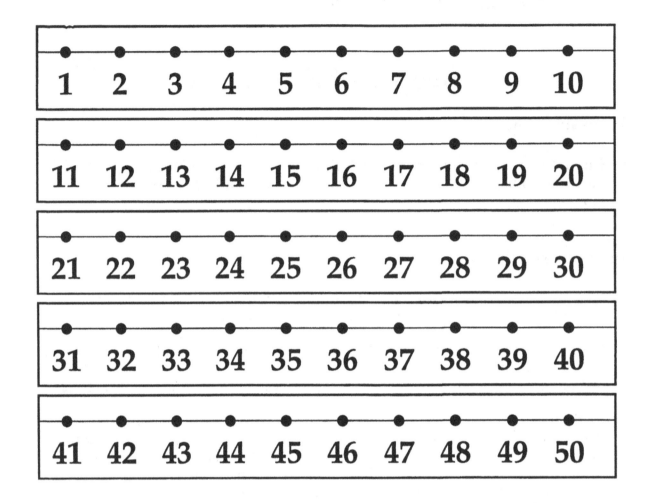

*Cut apart and assemble with tape – add to page 131*

# "Keeper of the Secret" Number line (part 2)

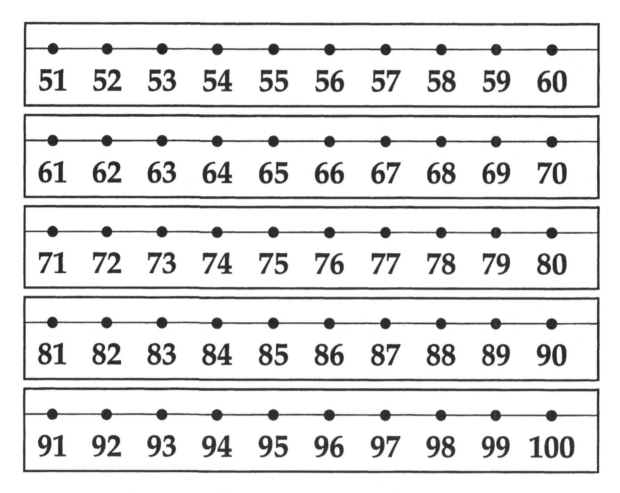

| 51 | 52 | 53 | 54 | 55 | 56 | 57 | 58 | 59 | 60 |

| 61 | 62 | 63 | 64 | 65 | 66 | 67 | 68 | 69 | 70 |

| 71 | 72 | 73 | 74 | 75 | 76 | 77 | 78 | 79 | 80 |

| 81 | 82 | 83 | 84 | 85 | 86 | 87 | 88 | 89 | 90 |

| 91 | 92 | 93 | 94 | 95 | 96 | 97 | 98 | 99 | 100 |

*Cut apart and assemble with tape – add to page 130*

# Round-Off Raceway

## Preparation:

- Make a copy of page 135 for each group of students.

- Provide groups of students with 2 small containers. Place 0-9 tiles in each container. Label one container "Tens" and the other container "Ones."

- Game markers

## Procedure:

- Provide the groups with the materials listed above. Ask the students to place the tiles facedown in the containers.

- The students place the game marker on the word START.

- The first student draws one tile each from the Tens and the Ones container. You may signal this by saying, "Draw One."

- The first student rounds the number drawn to the nearest ten. He or she places the game marker on the rounded number that is on the **Round-Off Raceway** game mat.

- All students in the group take a turn, following this procedure.

- The first student draws from the containers again and rounds the number. If the answer is ahead of the student on the game mat, he or she can move to that position on the mat. If the answer is behind the student, he or she cannot move until the next turn. All students in the group take a turn, following this procedure.

- The winner is the student who reaches the finish line first.

- Variations of this game can easily be made by adding hundreds and thousands and by changing the numbers on the game mat.

# Round-Off Raceway

## NUMERATION CONCEPT:
*Rounding whole numbers to the nearest ten*

# Rounding Bingo

## Preparation:

- Reproduce Bingo Cards from pages 137-138.

- Provide game markers.

- Prepare playing cards numbers 0-99. Note: The **Up and Down River cards** on pages 48-56 are suitable for this game.

## Procedure:

- Distribute Bingo cards and game markers to each student.

- Draw a card from the deck and ask each student to round the number to the nearest ten. The student then covers that number on the card.

- The winner is the first student to get 5 in a row.

- Blank Bingo cards are provided on page 138. These cards could contain numbers that are multiples of 100 or 1,000 for a more advanced version of Bingo.

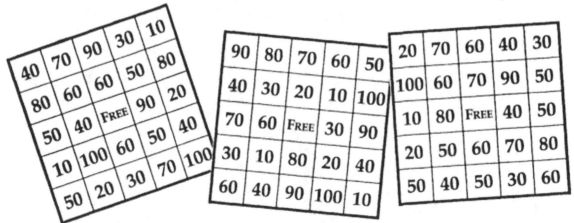

# Bingo Cards

| 40 | 80 | 10 | 60 | 20 |
|----|----|----|----|----|
| 10 | 70 | 100 | 30 | 80 |
| 50 | 30 | FREE | 90 | 40 |
| 20 | 100 | 50 | 70 | 10 |
| 90 | 60 | 30 | 80 | 50 |

| 40 | 70 | 90 | 30 | 10 |
|----|----|----|----|----|
| 80 | 60 | 60 | 50 | 80 |
| 50 | 40 | FREE | 90 | 20 |
| 10 | 100 | 60 | 50 | 40 |
| 50 | 20 | 30 | 70 | 100 |

| 20 | 100 | 30 | 80 | 90 |
|----|-----|----|----|----|
| 10 | 20 | 70 | 50 | 30 |
| 40 | 60 | FREE | 80 | 90 |
| 30 | 10 | 30 | 70 | 100 |
| 20 | 100 | 90 | 30 | 60 |

| 20 | 70 | 60 | 40 | 30 |
|----|----|----|----|----|
| 100 | 60 | 70 | 90 | 50 |
| 10 | 80 | FREE | 40 | 50 |
| 20 | 50 | 60 | 70 | 80 |
| 50 | 40 | 50 | 30 | 60 |

| 30 | 50 | 70 | 10 | 100 |
|----|----|----|----|-----|
| 80 | 40 | 20 | 90 | 30 |
| 10 | 80 | FREE | 40 | 60 |
| 20 | 50 | 10 | 70 | 90 |
| 100 | 60 | 30 | 50 | 80 |

| 90 | 80 | 70 | 60 | 50 |
|----|----|----|----|----|
| 40 | 30 | 20 | 10 | 100 |
| 70 | 60 | FREE | 30 | 90 |
| 30 | 10 | 80 | 20 | 40 |
| 60 | 40 | 90 | 100 | 10 |

# Bingo Cards

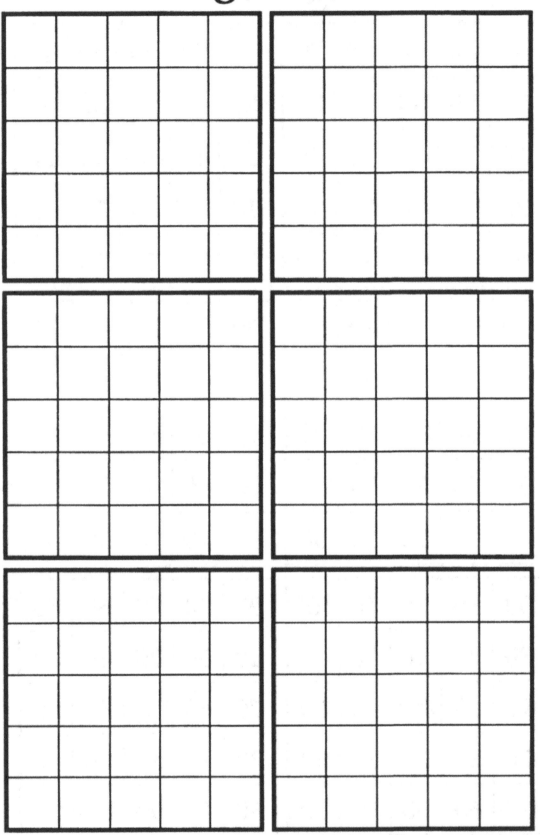

# Answer Keys

1. A. 9
4
5

B. 6
2
3

C. 1
8
7

2. A. 5
6
1

B. 4
9
3

C. 7
8
2

3. A. 2
5
4

B. 6
3
0

C. 9
7
1

4. A. 7
0
2

5. B. 5
9
3

C. 3
1
6

6. A. 7
2
3

B. 4
9
5

C. 0
1
6

7. A. 1
9
8

B. 3
7
2

C. 5
4
0

1. A. 1
6
2

B. 4
3
8

C. 7
5
9

2. A. 5
8
3

B. 4
7
6

C. 0
2
1

3. A. 3
7
2

B. 8
4
0

C. 1
5
9

4. A. 2
0
9

B. 3
5
7

C. 4
6
8

5. A. 2
7
3

B. 4
6
1

C. 9
8
5

6. A. 1
2
7

B. 4
3
0

C. 8
5
6

1. A. 6
3
2
4

B. 0
1
5
9

2. A. 1
2
4
7

B. 3
9
5
6

3. A. 6
0
3
4

B. 1
9
7
5

4. A. 4
2
3
1

B. 6
7
8
5

5. A. 9
0
1
7

B. 4
6
5
2

6. A. 8
6
9
3

B. 2
4
1
7

7. A. 2
7
6
1

B. 0
9
8
3

8. A. 9
6
7

5

B. 1
3
4
2

PAGE 68

1. A. 0
2
1
6
B. 5
4
9
3

2. A. 7
1
2
8
B. 0
9
3
4

3. A. 1
2
4
7
B. 8
0
3
5

4. A. 8
9
2
1
B. 7
4
6
3

5. A. 6
9
4
2
B. 5
0
1
3

6. A. 6
8
7
9

7. A. 2
7
6
1
B. 9
8
3
4

8. A. 0
4
2
8

B. 5
3
1
0

PAGE 70

1. 6
3
5
2
9
4

2. 2
6
4
3
8
1

3. 6
3
2
1
5
4

4. 6
0
2
1
3
5

5. 3
7
1
2
5

4
6. 5
6
1
2
7
9

7. 5
2
4
3
6
1

8. 9
0
7
1
5
6

PAGE 71

1. 6
0
4
7
3
1

2. 4
6
2
9
8
3

3. 9
3
7
5
0
1

4. 5
3
7
2
4
6

5. 4
0
2
1
7
5

6. 6
1
2
4
5
9

7. 7
0
5
3
9
4

8. 1
8
0
6
2

9
PAGE 73

1. 2
5
3
0
1
4
6

2. 4
1
0
6
3
5
7

3. 0
3
1
5
4
2
9

4. 9
0
4
3
1
6
2

5. 2
1
3
7
8
9

0
6. 3
9
2
1
6
7
5

7. 9
8
2
6
5
1
4

8. 0
1
9
7
2
3
6

PAGE 74

1. 5
7
2
6
4
1
3

2. 6
8
1
4
9
2

3
3. 5
3
8
4
6
9
7

4. 5
2
0
4
3
1
7

5. 0
5
4
3
8
2
6

6. 3
7
1
4
8
9
2

7. 2
1
7
8
0
5
3

8. 9
4
3
2
7
1
5

PAGE 76

1. 8
4 5
3 2
7 1
9 6

2. 9
1 7
2 6
0 5
4 3

3. 2
0 3
6 5
1 4
9 7

4. 4
3 7
1 8
5 2
6 0

5. 8
4 1
5 6
3 7

9    2

PAGE 77

1. 6
   8    1
   3    7
   2    4
   5    9

2. 1
   2    3
   4    8
   9    0
   7    6

3. 0
   2    5
   7    6
   3    1
   4    9

4. 2
   6    9
   5    4
   7    3
   1    8

5. 8
   6    7
   5    4
   1    9
   0    2

PAGE 80

1. A. 193
   B. 625

C. 478
2. A. 621
   B. 095
   C. 347

3. A. 204
   B. 137
   C. 659

4. A. 496
   B. 123
   C. 508

5. A. 730
   B. 156
   C. 248

PAGE 81

1. A. 562
   B. 104
   C. 987

2. A. 432
   B. 105
   C. 967

3. A. 900
   B. 531
   C. 724

4. A. 004
   B. 329
   C. 168

5. A. 017
   B. 806

C. 923

PAGE 83

1. A. 1,492
   B. 3,867

2. A. 6,732
   B. 5,401

3. A. 9,003
   B. 2,157

4. A. 3,620
   B. 5,310

5. A. 4,310
   B. 7,259

6. A. 2,015
   B. 3,749

PAGE 85

1. 459,270

2. 523,460

3. 948,321

4. 854,607

5. 320,549

6. 205,867

7. 153,496

8. 792,501

9. 640,013

10. 320,015

PAGE 87

1. 405,239,871

2. 897,653,012

3. 609,341,578

4. 029,875,146

5. 732,064,518

PAGE 97

1. A. 4
      6
      8
      9

   B. 7
      2
      1
      3

2. A. 5
      6
      0
      1

   B. 3
      2
      7
      4

3. A. 2
      3
      1

         9

   B. 6
      5
      8
      4

4. A. 3
      9
      2
      8

   B. 7
      4
      0
      6

PAGE 99

A. 4  6
   9  7
   8  3

B. 3  4
   2  1
   6  7

PAGE 101

A. 4  1
   3  5
   9  7
   2

B. 2
   6  4
   3  8
   9  1

PAGE 103

5    3
0    8
7    9
6
4
2

PAGE 117

1. A. 107
   B. 345
   C. 987
   D. 600

2. A. 075
   B. 296
   C. 401
   D. 308

3. A. 960
   B. 803
   C. 752
   D. 041

4. A. 107
   B. 250
   C. 308
   D. 469

1. A. 5,210
   B. 4,309
   C. 7,680

2. A. 9,703
   B. 6,042
   C. 8,501

3. A. 5,001
   B. 2,346
   C. 7,980

4. A. 3,020
   B. 1,297
   C. 6,048

5. A. 2,109
   B. 7,085
   C. 6,034

6. A. 6,139
   B. 4,070
   C. 8,025

PAGE 121

1. A. 130,068
   B. 240,579

2. A. 980,765
   B. 400,321

3. A. 123,098

B. 756,004

4. A. 509,402
   B. 107,638

5. A. 532,178
   B. 900,046

6. A. 405,790
   B. 132,068

PAGE 123

1. 1,546,703

2. 9,705,218

3. 1,357,924

4. 3,250,698

5. 4,600,012

6. 8,001,234

7. 1,543,000

8. 6,573,210

9. 4,095,801

10. 1,002,034

Dr. Kathleen Fletcher Bacer is currently a professor and creator/director of Azusa Pacific University's Online Master of Arts in Educational Technology Program. Her expertise stems from 19 years of K-8 classroom teaching and training teachers in classroom management and manipulative math techniques. Daughter of a retired innovative science teacher, mother of 3 daughters, and "nana" to Avalon Jean, her teaching models a belief that "critical to any teaching/learning process is the ability to effectively connect with the learner enabling them to construct a personal educational experience." As a mathematics teacher nominee of the year (1984), Dodger Education Hero Award (1991), Good Apple Award (1993), Teacher of the Year (1995-1996), and in the Who's Who Among Americas Teachers (2004-08), she is known for her innovative and creative techniques.

ISBN 142514575-2